Business

by **ALDEN GUILD, J. D.,** *in collaboration*

with DEANE C. DAVIS *and* DAVID F. HOXIE

NATIONAL LIFE INSURANCE

Partnership

Purchase

Agreements

COMPANY, MONTPELIER, VERMONT

Fourth Edition 1984

1st Printing, December 1962
2nd Printing-r, September 1967

2nd Edition, March 1973
3rd Edition, September 1978
2nd Printing, September 1979
3rd Printing, November 1980

4th Edition, November 1984

Foreword

FOR MANY YEARS National Life Insurance Company has realized the valuable function which life insurance can perform in many business arrangements. It has been a leader in trying to help its field forces, businessmen and their attorneys to recognize business situations in which life insurance can be useful and to arrange the insurance indicated in such a manner as to serve best the particular business need involved.

Back in the middle 30's George B. Young, then Vice President and General Counsel of National Life Insurance Company, wrote and published a book entitled "Business Insurance." In 1945, when Deane C. Davis succeeded to Mr. Young's position with the Company, he expanded on Mr. Young's work by writing and publishing a booklet entitled "Life Insurance and Business Purchase Agreements." Still later, in 1948, Mr. Davis prepared an enlarged second edition in book form. Then, in 1960, and since so many changes had taken place in the way in which business is transacted and in the tax laws affecting business transactions, and because the life insurance industry had itself made so much progress in developing new and different ways in which life insurance can serve the businessman, it became necessary again to revise Mr. Davis' work completely.

Mr. Alden Guild of the Company's Law Department was authorized to undertake the production of a series of books covering various topics in the area of business insurance. Mr. Guild is a graduate of Dartmouth College and the University of Chicago Law School, was a Managing Editor of its Law Review and a member of both Phi Beta Kappa and the Order of the Coif. He is now Vice President and General Counsel of the Company.

"Stock-Purchase Agreements and The Close Corporation," represented the first step in 1960, followed in 1961 by "Professional Partnership Purchase Plans" and in 1962 by "Business-Partnership Purchase Agreements." These books have been widely distributed — about 250,000 copies to date — and they have received much favorable comment. We are, therefore, all the more pleased at this point in time to offer this fourth edition.

November 1984

RICHARD I. FRICKE

President

Contents

Citations

Cases

Internal Revenue Code of 1954 — Sections

Preface

THIS BOOK has been published in order to help lawyers, accountants, trust officers and life underwriters assist their clients in the formation of effective business-purchase agreements. Its purpose is not to give legal advice. Rather, this book should vividly demonstrate that the active participation of the client's own legal counsel is absolutely and undeniably essential. This fact is certainly pointed up dramatically by a reading of the chapter entitled "Tax Considerations" which should serve as plain warning to the uninitiated that there can be no substitute for competent, professional advice. We hope, however, that this book will be useful to lawyers who are in private practice and who may not deal in this particular area of law daily. No attempt has been made herein to make ultimate conclusions for the parties involved; rather, we have attempted to provide some basic analyses with which the decision-making function can, hopefully, be made more effective.

The outline of this book, like its predecessors in the series, is really quite simple. First, we show why a purchase plan may be desirable. Second, the types of plans available are indicated, their advantages as well as their shortcomings, and the problem of valuation is also considered. Then, we analyze the tax consequences of the various transactions, and, finally, we provide specimen agreements which may contain some valuable guideposts for the lawyers involved.

What is a Business Partnership?

"A ROSE IS A ROSE IS A ROSE." That might satisfy the curiosity of a poetess, but if horticulturists are at all like lawyers, they would certainly take issue with such a general proposition. Few lawyers would agree that "a partnership is a partnership is a partnership." True, the legal framework of one partnership is more like another than unlike, and it is a simple matter to find characteristics common to all.

Liability of general partners, for example, or fiduciary obligations among them are but two similar threads in the fabric of all partnerships. So also the joint nature of ownership of partnership property as well as the existence of a profit motive.

Differences, however, of a substantial nature can be found in the kind of business that is carried on. Generally speaking, a partnership sells one of two things: services or products. Naturally, one can think of several lines of business which involve both a service and a product. A partnership of doctors, for example, primarily sells service; it would be unusual if a medical partnership carried a pharmaceutical inventory of medicines, surgical supplies and the like. A pharmaceutical partnership, on the other hand, receives its income *primarily* from the sale of products, even though skilled personal services are certainly fundamental to the success of the business.

Existence of an inventory, then, would appear to be a relatively simple distinction among partnerships. Professional or personal-service partnerships on the one hand, product or business-type partnerships on the other.

Note, however, another difference which is commonly found in partnership situations, and observe that there appears to be a high degree of correlation between the two differences. Generally speaking, *service* partnerships have larger amounts of unrealized receivables proportionately than *product* partnerships. As a matter of fact, the unrealized receivables of a service partnership can form the largest single item of value to the partnership (aside from the partners themselves, of course), while the inventory, or tangible stock in trade, of a product partnership constitutes the chief asset.

A convenient way to categorize a personal-service firm is to call it a "professional partnership," e.g., doctors, lawyers and the like. Shorthand designation of a product firm is to call it a "business partnership," e.g., hardware or appliance store, food market, etc. When using these brief names to describe a particular type of partnership, there should be no implication that a *professional* partnership is "superior" to a *business* partnership; whether a partnership is "professional" in the *ethical* sense of that word is a matter which is largely up to the individual partners.

Why Plan?

AT LEAST a few employees enjoy the dubious luxury of being able to slumber deep within the framework of large corporations, but *partners* in relatively small businesses are usually compelled, like it or not, to toil long and hard for their bread. A partner wears two hats — he is, as a practical matter, both employer *and* employee. Consequently, it seems quite tragic when a partner helps to build up a business "inch by inch" only to have his lifelong efforts vanish for little or naught because of his failure to peer briefly into the future and to participate in some basic planning.

Look, for example, at the case of Peters' Peerless Pharmacy, currently owned and operated by Andy Peters, Norm Morton and Fred Flanders. Peters acquired the business — originally "Deane's Drugs" — from the Estate of Lewis Deane shortly after his discharge from the service in 1962. Peters went to work for Deane as a *very* junior associate exactly nine months to the day before Deane (who had hitherto always worn bow ties) managed to get his Christmas four-in-hand caught in the centrifuge, and thereupon, observe it tighten around his neck at a slightly faster pace than he could loosen it. It did not take Peters too awfully long after Deane's unexpected demise to think how nice it would be to own the drugstore outright, but lacking what he considered to be sufficient funds, he was sorely tempted to take a job with a large chain of drugstores operating in neighboring cities. However, with no other licensed pharmacist in town, how could Mrs. Deane quickly liquidate her late husband's business? Because of the unavoidable impatience for cash evidenced by Deane's necessitous widow, the result was simply that a "sacrifice" price was all that Peters had to pay, in spite of Deane's lifelong investment of time, money and effort in the store. Even though the amount finally paid to Mrs. Deane was a mere fraction of what the cost would have been under auspicious circumstances, Peters was compelled to mortgage everything he owned at nearly usurious rates, as well as to petition family and friends for rather sizable loans. As a result of his large over-all indebtedness, Peters was soon eager to take into partnership two neighbors of his, Morton and Flanders, who were financially able to contribute to capital. This was a step which he otherwise would not have taken inasmuch as his new colleagues seemed allergic to work and since the business at the time was capable of adequately supporting only two men.

Disappointed was the word for *both* Mrs. Deane and Mr. Peters. How could either of them be satisfied with what had taken place: (1) She wound up with *less* than full value for her husband's business, and (2) he was saddled with *more* of a debt than he could comfortably carry.

Eventually, however, Mr. Peters' financial picture and the economic soundness of the drugstore improved considerably through much hard labor on his part and because of an increasing attention to work displayed by his two partners. The business grew and by 1972 the fair market value of each partner's share of the business was as follows:

Peters — 40% — $48,000
Morton — 30% — $36,000
Flanders — 30% — $36,000

While a reasonable portion of the value was attributable to good will, the major part came from stock in trade, the building and the fixtures. The corner location, the modern equipment in the soda fountain area, the pharmaceutical equipment, including a new and safer centrifuge — all of these things added up to wealth, albeit modest.

Needless to say, it became increasingly necessary to conserve and to protect this growing wealth. So long as all three partners remained loyal to each other and healthy, there would be no substantial worry. But Peters especially knew what his own widow might be left with upon *his* death if he showed no more foresight than his unenlightened predecessor. He knew that there must be a better way to cope with *inevitable* changes than simply to leave their outcome to Lady Luck, who had been so fickle to the Deanes.

Generally speaking, Andy Peters and his two associates needed two things to make their future and the future of their business secure. (1) A Plan. (2) Money. If Lewis Deane had had a plan with Peters, then it would have been clear who the buyer of the drugstore was to be from the moment Deane died. And if Peters had had sufficient money, instead of a heavy mortgage and a barrage of installment payments to make, it would have been equally obvious where the money was that should have been paid to Deane's widow as quickly as checks could be written.

Unless a partner or his partnership happens to be appreciably richer than average, he or the partnership (depending upon what sort of business-purchase plan fits the situation) will most likely be inclined to use life insurance as the medium to fund the plan. While it is certainly true that savings which are regularly deposited and not withdrawn can grow year by year, there is no kind of property, aside from life insurance, which can provide *complete* funding from the very instant the business-purchase agreement is executed. Certainly, there is nothing magic about the use of life insurance to fund business-purchase agreements, but there is indeed much to commend life insurance as the only *practical* funding vehicle.

Inasmuch as discussion about the variety, desirability and usefulness of life insurance contracts should understandably be led by the life underwriter, this book will be confined by and large to the subject of the business-purchase plan or agreement itself, resting on the assumption that the parties to a particular agreement will be properly advised as to life insurance by a competent life underwriter.

Laying aside, then, the question of the funding method, how does one know what sort of plan should be chosen in order to provide adequate machinery to effectuate the exchange of money for the business interests? Should the partners agree among only themselves to buy each other out upon the death or disability of one of them, or should the partnership — as an entity — be made to purchase a decedent or disabled partner's interest? Or, perhaps, some combination or variation of a "classic" pattern?

Determination of an answer to some of these questions should be made easier by the discussion contained in the next chapter.

The Plans —
Entity Purchase
or Cross Purchase

ENTITY PURCHASE AND CROSS PURCHASE — these are the two classic kinds of buy-out plans. Indeed, these are available whether the business is a corporation or a partnership. And it is entirely possible to stray from well-traveled paths and to use a variant of one of these agreements or a combination of the two. Let us, however, examine the basic outline of each approach.

ENTITY PURCHASE

If you are familiar with the skeleton of a corporation's stock-retirement or stock-redemption agreement, then you are at once knowledgeable with respect to a partnership entity-purchase plan. Customarily, the entity-purchase contract requires *the partnership* to buy (and the estate to sell) the partnership interests of a deceased partner. The funding insurance, on the life of the deceased partner, is owned, purchased by and payable to the partnership. Consequently, if there are three partners, the partnership would own an insurance policy on the life of each partner with itself as beneficiary in order to be assured of having funds available to pay the estate in accordance with the terms of the entity-purchase agreement.

Another question frequently arises in discussing the entity-purchase plan: What is a partnership *entity?* Traditionally, a partner-

Illustration of an Entity-Purchase Plan

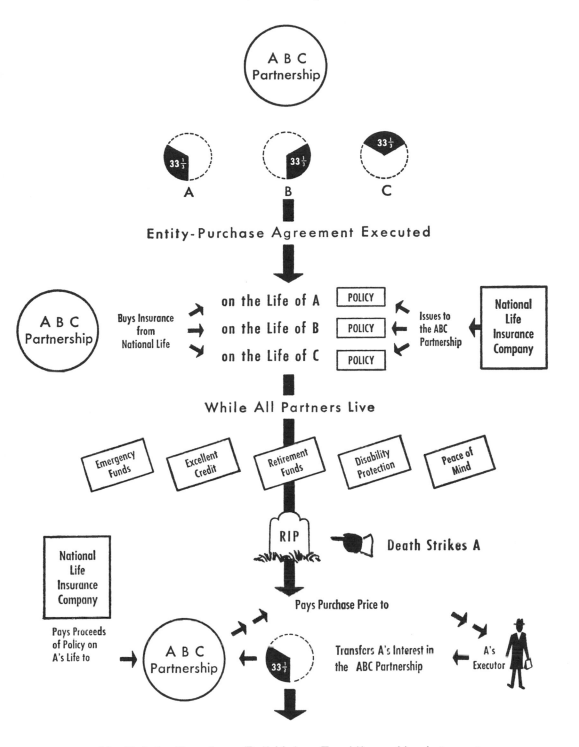

A's Estate Receives Full Value For His or Her Interest
AND
B and C Own The Entire Partnership

ship has not been viewed by lawyers as a legal unit like a corporation.* Rather, a partnership has been usually treated as an aggregation of mutual agents without a separate "body" apart from them. A corporation, on the other hand, is a distinct legal unit apart from its shareholders, directors and employees; it, for example, not the president, is the employer of the persons working for it. Unfortunately, then, there is no clear-cut answer to this question except to say that it is largely sufficient for our purposes to realize that in recent years it has, in certain instances, become acceptable to view the partnership as an entity. This is especially so in matters of taxation by the federal government.

CROSS PURCHASE

This sort of agreement is, perhaps, a bit easier to understand. Each partner agrees with the other partners that upon his death his share of the partnership will be sold to the surviving partners, or that upon the death of another partner he will purchase a proportionate part of such deceased's interest in the partnership. When life insurance is used to fund a contract such as this, each partner buys insurance made payable to himself on the life of each of his co-partners. Thus, in the case of three partners, A owns a policy on B and a policy on C, B on A and C, and C on A and B. As discussed below, of course, the contingency which prompts purchase does not have to be death alone; disability or retirement is also available.

CONTINGENCIES OF PURCHASE

More often than not the contingency upon which the purchase agreement is triggered is the *death* of a partner. This need not be the only contingency, however. Normal retirement at 65 or total and permanent disability are two other events which may prompt a purchase, if the agreement is so drawn. If the obligation of the partnership can mature at a time sooner than death, the funding of the agreement becomes somewhat more complex. Suppose, for example, the purchase provision can be ignited by a partner's total and permanent disability;

---

* This is not entirely true, however. See, e.g., DUNBAR v. FARNUM & WIFE, 109 Vt. 313, 321; 196 Atl. 237, 240 (1937), and BROOKS v. ULANET, 116 Vt. 49; 69 A.2d 701 (1949).

Illustration of a Cross-Purchase Plan

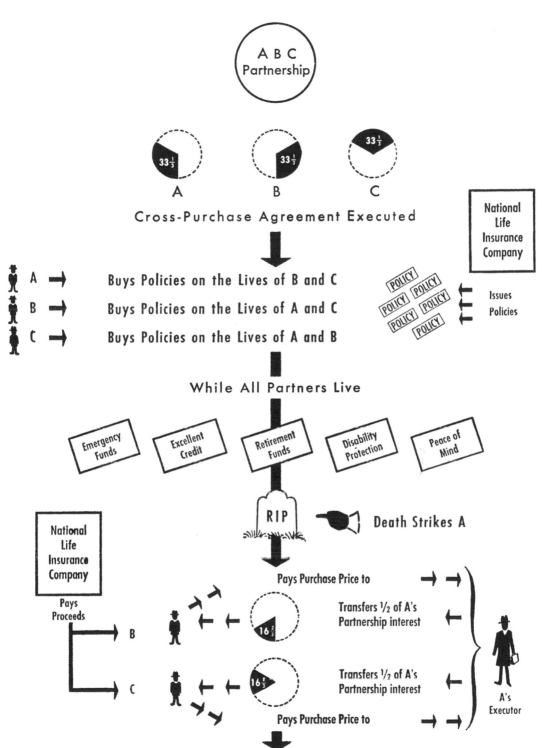

A's Estate Receives Full Value For His or Her Interest
AND
B and C Own The Entire Partnership

in such event it would appear rather necessary for the partnership to own disability insurance on the partners. Some life insurance companies issue policies designed to fund purchase agreements. A key consideration to remember while drafting the buy-out agreement is to make certain that the definition or "test" of disability be at least as strict as the one used in the funding disability insurance policy; in that way you avoid the financially disastrous picture of having a partner disabled enough to be bought out but yet not sufficiently disabled to cause the insurance company to pay off on its policy to the purchaser. One additional factor especially bears watching with regard to a purchase plan that is set into motion by a partner's disability. That is simply this: merely because a partner becomes disabled, and qualifies for insurance purposes for disability income, does not necessarily mean that he will *remain* so disabled until he dies or until he has been fully paid for his interest in the partnership. If the disabled partner, to whom installment payments are being made in exchange for or in liquidation of his interest in the partnership, regains his health, what to do? Perhaps a palatable solution would include one or more of the following ideas: (1) Provide in the agreement that a partner's disability must persist for a substantial period of time, such as 18 months to two years, even though the "waiting period" or qualifying time in the funding insurance may be comparatively minimal, e.g., three to six months; this would have the effect of ignoring extended illnesses which in fact are not really *permanent*. (2) Spread the purchase price on an installment basis for a longer rather than a shorter time. (3) And, perhaps in connection with (2), provide in the agreement that if disability-income payments by the insurer to the policyowner cease, then even more spread out installments (and thus smaller payments) will be permitted. It would not appear to be a wise move to call off the ball game once the buy-out has started unless it is in the very early innings.

With the broad outline of each plan in mind, what are some of the considerations which may prompt some partners to choose one method, some to choose another?

Advantages of the Entity-Purchase Method.

(1) Funding an entity-purchase agreement with life insurance is about as simple as can be, at least from the standpoint of the number of policies involved. If there are five partners, for example, there are only five insurance policies. In the case of cross-purchase funding there

would be, with five partners, twenty policies. This simplicity is desirable for two reasons. First, administration with respect to the application and payment for five policies is certainly much easier than when twenty are involved. Second, to the extent an insurer grades premiums by size (like economy-size buying), it may be considerably less expensive to restrict the number of policies.

(2) Where the partnership owns the funding policies, the loan values in the policies can be immediately and easily available to the partnership should it face some pressing business need. An emergency fund is thus built up automatically when the partnership funds an entity-purchase plan — a reserve for a "rainy day."

(3) If the partners' ages are widely divergent and if the younger partner simply cannot pay the higher premiums required for the insurance on the older life, funding by the partnership can ease his burden; premium payments would, for purposes of determining distributive shares, be accounted for as expenses of the partnership. Indeed, under such an accounting procedure the older partner would, to a certain extent, be helping to buy himself out, but the advantages of having a workable purchase plan — a plan which can hold great attraction especially to the older partner — serve to make such equalization of premium payments palatable to him. It should be borne in mind that this equalization of premium payments does not necessarily have to occur when funding an entity-purchase plan; a skillfull accountant can, no doubt, develop a formula for a given situation which would result in an exact charge to each partner for the insurance protection he receives.

Disadvantages of the Entity-Purchase Method.

(1) The problem of "ballooning" — which is present within corporate stock-retirement plans — is also present in a partnership entity-purchase arrangement. At the outset, though, it should be noted that as a practical matter the problem of ballooning usually does not, standing alone, deter partners from choosing the entity-purchase approach. To illustrate ballooning let us assume the ABC partnership has total net assets of $60,000; A, B, and C are equal co-partners, each owning a $20,000 (one-third) interest. The object, if A should die, is to pay A's estate his one-third value, $20,000, and yet keep a $60,000 partnership for B and C without having to liquidate any of the firm's assets. If the partnership purchases a $20,000 policy on A's life, at A's

death it certainly would have the liquid funds needed to pay off its contractual obligation to A's estate and B and C would end up with a partnership totaling $60,000 in assets. But — and watch closely — at the
moment of A's death, the partnership is suddenly worth $80,000
because of the $20,000 due from and payable by the insurance com-
pany. If A's estate is to receive his *full* one-third interest in the partnership, should not the payment be $26,666.67? But, if the answer is affir-
mative and if the partnership does make such a payment, then it would
be necessary to liquidate $6,666.67 worth of partnership assets, and B
and C would wind up with a partnership worth only $53,333.33.
Various "solutions" are available to alleviate the problem of ballooning. Perhaps the most popular approach is to specify in the valuation
or price provision of the buy-out agreement that the cash surrender
value of the policy as of the moment before the insured's death should
be included, but not the total proceeds; and it will be observed that
this is an approach made available in the specimen agreements at the
end of this text. Another solution is to ignore the problem. This is not
as foolhardy (or as facetious) as one might think, especially where the
three partners are of nearly equal age and in the same condition of
health; in such a case each one is simply betting that he will not be the
first to die and is willing to risk a loss if it should turn out differently.
Another solution is to "fund to the maximum," i.e., purchase enough
insurance so that two-thirds of the partnership's value at A's death will
equal the original value, namely $60,000. Thus $30,000 of insurance
would be purchased on each partner's life, not $20,000. Now if A
dies, the partnership will be worth $90,000, his one-third will be
$30,000, and B and C end up with the full $60,000 partnership. Still
another solution is to hedge — to fund beyond the minimum
($20,000) but not to the maximum ($30,000).

(2) Upon purchase by the partnership of the decedent partner's interest in the partnership the tax or cost basis of the surviving
partners does not increase as would be the case under a cross-purchase
agreement. "Basis" is important in determining gain (or loss) which
may result from later sales by the survivors. Section 705(a) of the 1954
Code provides that the adjusted basis of a partner's interest in a partnership shall be the basis of such interest determined under Section 722
(relating to contributions to a partnership) or Section 742 (relating to
transfers of partnership interests), increased by the sum of his
distributive share of the partnership's income (including its tax-exempt
income for the taxable year and prior taxable years) and decreased by

partnership distributions to him as well as by the sum of his distributive share of partnership losses for the taxable year and prior taxable years. Insurance proceeds are exempt from income taxation under Section 101(a). Consequently, if the ABC partnership receives upon *A*'s death $30,000 of insurance which is owned on his life (each partner owning an equal share in the partnership), there would be an increase in the cost basis of each partner equal to $10,000. If, on the other hand, there were a cross-purchase agreement, and *B* and *C* each owned $15,000 worth of insurance on *A*'s life, each would receive on *A*'s death $15,000 which, when used to purchase *A*'s interest in the partnership, would increase the basis of each in the new partnership by $15,000. If and when *B* or *C* later sells his partnership interest during his lifetime, then the larger basis would be welcomed. It should be remembered that under the entity-purchase method each of the three equal partners pays only one-third of the premiums on each policy, whereas under the cross-purchase arrangement each partner individually pays the entire premiums on the policies he owns on his colleagues' lives. The partnership agreement can provide that the policy proceeds are to be credited only to the accounts of the surviving partners. See Code Section 704. Such a provision would increase *B*'s and *C*'s basis for their respective interests in the partnership by $15,000.

(3) Another possible drawback to the entity plan can be observed in those situations where the partnership is likely to become very much indebted. Creditors, levying upon the partnership's assets, can clearly reach the policy values. Actually, however, this disadvantage should not, as a practical matter, scare partnerships away from entity purchase. General partners are at least jointly liable for the obligations and wrongful acts of the partnership, and this liability stretches beyond each partner's capital interest in the partnership; thus, even in a cross-funded purchase plan the insurance policies would be vulnerable to creditor attack.

Advantages of the Cross-Purchase Method.

(1) Simplicity is also one of the advantageous hallmarks of the cross-purchase method, albeit a different kind of simplicity than that found in the entity-purchase arrangement. It appears that some people understandably have difficulty in appreciating what actually happens when the partnership buys out a partner's interest; the same people, however, usually grasp quite clearly and quickly what transpires in a

cross-purchase plan. The concept of the entity is not needed here, and each partner can observe *directly* what *he* is buying or selling, both with respect to interests in the partnership and to the funding insurance. And if businessmen are to be urged into entering some sort of business-purchase arrangement, then it is indeed valuable for them to understand what is going on — this should not be a deep, dark secret among the lawyer, life underwriter and accountant.

(2) Another possible advantage under the cross-purchase set-up is that each partner buys only the amount of insurance he needs on the lives of his co-partners. Unlike entity purchase, there is no ballooning. Further, there is no automatic equalization of premium payments. In addition, if a partner happens to be fortunate enough to have liquid assets of his own outside the partnership which could in part be used to fund his obligations under the plan, he could under-fund to a point satisfactory to him and his colleagues.

Disadvantages of the Cross-Purchase Method.

(1) If a partnership is composed of a great many members, then quite clearly the funding of a cross-purchase plan can become quite a complex and burdensome affair. If, for example, there are five partners, twenty policies of life insurance would be required*; under an entity-purchase plan only five would be needed.

(2) If it is contemplated that after the first partner dies the survivors will enter into another buy-out agreement, then there would be greater administrative difficulty in a cross-purchase situation, where there would be a need to transfer the unmatured policies owned by the decedent partner on the lives of his surviving colleagues. This particular difficulty is by no means insurmountable and fortunately does not present any tax problems, such as do exist in a similar situation involving stockholders of a corporation.

(3) The creditors of a profligate partner may seize the policies which he owns on his partner's lives in order to satisfy his personal debts to them. Since each partner relies upon the other partners to carry the required amount of insurance on his life and thus obtain the funds to purchase his partnership interest, the loss of policies to a partner's creditors could indeed prove to be serious.

---

* Consult, however, the chapter entitled "Use of a Trustee."

(4) Another disadvantage, but again of a non-fatal variety, is the need for the surviving partners to remember to make an election under Section 754 of the 1954 Internal Revenue Code, as discussed under "Tax Considerations."

Transfer-for-Value Rule.

In (2) immediately above reference was made to the fact that no tax problem would be encountered should A's estate sell his policy on B to C and on C to B. If the partnership were not a partnership but a corporation, such assignments of the policies would result in dire consequences — the transfers would collide head-on with Section 101(a)(2) of the 1954 Internal Revenue Code.* The transfer-for-value rule states that if a life insurance policy is assigned for a valuable consideration, then upon maturity of the policy the assignee takes as his basis only that which he had actually paid for the policy (including net premiums paid), and the balance of the proceeds is taxable as ordinary income to him. Thus, the transfer-for-value rule is an exception to Section 101(a)(1) which grants a blanket of apparent immunity to life insurance proceeds from income taxation. The Code has, however, provided special haven to partners. Section (101)(2)(B) contains important exceptions to the transfer-for-value rule; the rule does not apply "if such transfer is to the insured, *to a partner of the insured, to a partnership in which the insured is a partner,* or to a corporation in which the insured is a shareholder or officer." This is important not only with respect to transfers which may take place after the first partner dies (in order to fund a successive buy-out agreement) but also with respect to the initial placement of the insurance policies. If, for example, in a corporate buy-out situation the funding policies are placed on a stock-retirement basis (corporation as owner) and it is later decided that

---

* Section 101 *** Transfer for Valuable Consideration. — In the case of a transfer for a valuable consideration, by assignment or otherwise, of a life insurance contract or any interest therein, the amount excluded from gross income by paragraph (1) shall not exceed an amount equal to the sum of the actual value of such consideration and the premiums and other amounts subsequently paid by the transferee. The preceding sentence shall not apply in the case of such a transfer —

(A) if such contract or interest therein has a basis for determining gain or loss in the hands of a transferee determined in whole or in part by reference to such basis of such contract or interest therein the hands of the transferor, or

(B) if such transfer is to the insured, to a partner of the insured, to a partnership in which the insured is a partner, or to a corporation in which the insured is a shareholder or officer.

cross purchase is indicated, then there is no way that the existing policies can be used to fund the cross-purchase arrangement without running smack dab into the transfer-for-value rule. Partners, however, are a "chosen people." In a like situation it would be perfectly all right for the partnership to assign for value existing policies to partners who are not the insured in such policies.

The Importance of Adhering to a Classic Arrangement.

It would be difficult to overemphasize the desirability of sticking to a usual pattern once one of the two approaches has been chosen. In this regard it may suffice to outline the facts and decision in LEGALLET V. COMMISSIONER, 41 B.T.A. 294 (1940); each of two partners took out an insurance policy on his own life with his wife as beneficiary, all in accordance with an agreement providing that the widow of the first partner to die should receive the policy proceeds as part payment for the decedent partner's interest in the partnership. Premium payments were made by the partnership and charged to the partners in equal shares. Ultimately, one of the partners died and the proceeds of his insurance policy were paid to his widow, notes being given for the balance of the agreed purchase price by the surviving partner. Subsequently, the surviving partner sold some of the assets of the partnership, and litigation then developed over the question of whether the insurance proceeds paid to the deceased partner's widow should be considered as part of the cost basis of the surviving partner in determining his gain or loss on the sale. The Board of Tax Appeals agreed with the Commissioner by holding that the insurance proceeds should not be so treated inasmuch as the surviving partner had not paid them to her and because the premiums on the policy had been paid by the partnership. Thus, the Board was unable to trace the payment of the policy proceeds to the survivor, i.e., it did not agree that the insurance company simply made the payments *on behalf of* the surviving partner. A more recent case, involving a similar factual situation, held the insurance company's payment to a deceased partner's widow to have been made, in effect, by the surviving partners because the designation of the partners' wives as beneficiaries of the policies on the partners' lives was only a security device. MUSHRO V. COMMISSIONER, 50 T.C. 43(1968). However, the Commissioner of Internal Revenue has announced that he will not follow MUSHRO. 1970/2 C. B. xxii. LEGALLET and the Commissioner's announcement with respect to

MUSHRO should stand as clear warning to adhere closely to the classic patterns of buy-out agreements. The well-settled and conservative approach to follow in a cross-purchase situation is to have the owner of each policy designated as beneficiary thereof and to have the buy-out agreement obligate him, not the insurance company, to pay the purchase price to the payee designated in the agreement independently of the receipt of insurance policy proceeds. Or, in the case of an entity-purchase agreement the partnership as owner should also be designated as beneficiary, and it, not the insurer, should pay the decedent partner's personal representative. While LEGALLET has been widely criticized, cautious attorneys continue to pay certain heed to it and to the Commissioner's position on MUSHRO.

Valuation

WHY IS IT "a must" to consider valuation in connection with business-partnership purchase agreements? Why is a price tag so important that we ask our printer to set an additional chapter of type?

A well-drawn price provision avoids haggling. The decedent partner's estate may expect to receive and the surviving partners may expect to pay a definitely determinable number of dollars for the business interest — no more, no less. While a tourist may find considerable stimulation in bargaining with street vendors at a bazaar, the picture changes materially when the surviving partners are confronted with a grieving widow. When there is a definite price, the purchase agreement can be executed promptly and without dispute — certainly a more tranquilizing prospect.

In addition, there is an advantage to be gained from definitely establishing price, which is invaluable to over-all financial and estate planning. If I am part owner of a partnership and if my interest in the business comprises a substantial portion of all my property, then how on earth can I know with reasonable assurance how much property is mine to give away at my death, by will or otherwise, without establishing the price? It may be that I am actually better off than I think, in which case I should have "remembered" more generously my church, college or favorite charity. On the other hand, I may overestimate my wealth, in which case my generosity to charity might result in a necessitous widow. Then, too, without an accurate valuation of my business interest, how can I predict the burden of death taxes and prepare sufficient liquid assets to meet it?

Another significant reason in favor of paying due attention to the price provision is that, if it is carefully drafted in the agreement, the value of the business interest will be pegged for estate-tax purposes. That is, the Internal Revenue Service will accept the value ascertained in the purchase agreement as the proper value to be inserted in the decedent partner's federal estate-tax return. Some people feel that *this reason alone* is sufficiently attractive to prompt businessmen to enter into business-purchase agreements, regardless of all the other advantages which accrue to the participants.

What are the characteristics of a well-drawn price provision which will peg the value of the business interest for federal estate-tax purposes? There are four:

First, the estate of the first to die must be obligated to sell the business interest.

Second, the partnership or the surviving partners must either be obligated to purchase the business interest of the decedent or be given an option to purchase that business interest.

Third, the agreement must forbid each participating partner from disposing of his interest during his lifetime without either the prior consent of the other partners or first offering it to the other partners or to the partnership at a price not higher than the price to be paid if the sale had been made by his estate to such other party.

Fourth, the agreement must be the result of an arm's-length transaction. This last requirement means simply that the price must have been arrived at in a business climate, that there must have been no intent to make a gift.

An especially significant case in this regard is FIORITO V. COM-MISSIONER, 33 T.C. 440 (1959), involving a partnership-purchase agreement which restricted the decedent's right to transfer his partnership interest during his lifetime and which also granted to the surviving partners an option to purchase his interest after death for its book value at the date of death. At Fiorito's death, the book value was *less* than its then fair market value. The Commissioner of Internal Revenue chose the latter — and higher — figure as the value which the executrix should have inserted in the estate-tax return; but the Tax Court found against him, holding that the purchase agreement was valid, was entered into to ensure the continuity of the business, that Fiorito was not during his lifetime at liberty to dispose of his partnership interest at a higher price without the consent of the other partners, and that as a consequence the price in the agreement should control. *See also* ESTATE OF BISCHOFF V. COMMISSIONER, 69 T.C. 32 (1977); BRODERICK V. GORE, 224 F.2d 892 (C.A. 10, 1955); ESTATE OF WEIL V. COMMISSIONER, 22 T.C. 1267 (1957).

What additional features distinguish a well-drawn price provision? There are several, but among them are the following:

GENUINENESS. If a formal approach is used, such as book value, capitalization of earnings or some combination of factors, care should be taken to avoid artificial results. Business accounts kept for tax purposes, for example, might reflect values which would diverge widely from what the interest would actually sell for on the market. How often are commercial buildings carried on the annual statement at $1? Then, too, book-value accounts are oftentimes not written up or down, as the case may be, to reflect changes in actual values since original acquisition.

UNDERSTANDABILITY. If only the attorney and the accountant, and not the partners themselves, understand the price provision, then a fertile seedbed for ultimate dissatisfaction and discord has almost certainly been planted. Moreover, the partners — the persons who presumably built the business and who are familiar with all aspects of it — should themselves participate in establishing the price, whatever method is finally chosen; no outsider can possibly have the owners' familiarity with a particular business, all its strengths and weaknesses, its sources and markets, its past and its prospects for the future. After all, one of the attractions of business-purchase agreements is the peace of mind made possible by the businessman's knowledge that his house is in order, that certain results will arise out of the uncertain future.

What are the methods commonly used to determine the price of a business interest? At this point in working out a business-purchase plan, an accountant can earn his fee many times over. Although he may have some personal preference as to the method of establishing value, he would probably agree that the following are among the most popular ways to set price:

(1) AGREED-DOLLAR VALUE. When the partners decide to use this method, the purchase agreement simply states the actual dollar

values agreed upon by the partners for the various partnership interests. In a very real sense this may not be a *method* of determining value inasmuch as it merely states a result; one of the partners may have arrived at the chosen figures by using book value, another by capitalization of earnings and a third by pure guesswork. Negotiation among the partners themselves is really the essence of this method, but it is negotiation while all of the partners are still alive, by the very persons who built the business, who are familiar with every facet of its past and potential growth, and who are the very ones, in the final analysis, who should be satisfied. If this method is used, then the partners should be careful to include a provision for mandatory periodic revaluations in order that appreciation or depreciation may be seasonably reflected in the agreement. And, for good measure, the agreement should call for some automatic revaluation by formula, or otherwise, in the event that the partners fail to observe their scheduled obligation to revalue the interests. The need for this latter safeguard is evident: If one of the partners becomes critically ill, for example, will his colleagues agree to raise the price in the case of great increase in value? Chances are they would be more than anxious to obtain a revaluation if a general recession occurred, but in such event the ill partner might be "too sick" to attend to his contractual duty to revalue. One possible disadvantage of the agreed-dollar approach could arise in a business partnership such as a drug, automotive supply or clothing store. These businesses will undoubtedly have an inventory of considerable, if not major, value, and some of the inventory may have a limited useful life where change in design or technological advance — or the passage of time itself — will take a rapid and devastating toll.

(2) BOOK VALUE. If the purchase price is to be established this way, then the value consists simply of the net assets of the partnership as reflected on its books. For book value to be considered fair, however, there should be some reasonable assurance that the books of the partnership state assets and liabilities truly, i.e., that assets are written up or down according to actual market value. Furthermore, the book-value approach will more often than not (and perhaps unintentionally) omit good will.

(3) CAPITALIZATION OF EARNINGS. When this method is used, the agreement provides that the average yearly net earnings for a certain number of prior years are to be capitalized at a stated interest percentage, depending upon the character of the business. A risky ven-

ture, for example, would call for a low one. The theory underlying this technique is that the measure of an asset's value is what it earns. With this in mind it should be abundantly clear that some adjustment must be made for the earnings attributable to services contributed by the partners themselves; certainly working partners contribute to the partnership earnings, and consequently it would seem mandatory to subtract from the average annual net earnings the amount fairly traceable to those services rendered. This involves guesswork, pure and simple, and so does the choice, really, of the rate of capitalization.

(4) POST-DEATH APPRAISAL. Occasionally, partners may be inclined to throw up their hands in despair over the problem of valuation and come to the conclusion that the matter could be resolved just as well by agreeing simply that certain persons, usually disinterested, should be appointed to appraise the value of the partnership after the death of the first partner. This arrangement has some appeal; no bothersome attention need be paid to the changing economic tides of the business during the life of the purchase agreement, and the impartiality that at least theoretically attends the appraisal method may be a source of considerable comfort. There are, however, some negatives in this method which, to some, seem to outweigh the positives. First, *accurate* funding would be difficult to achieve; the parties would not know the specific purchase price until one of the partners died. Second, a partner would be at a disadvantage in his personal estate planning; he would never really know how much *his* share of the business interest would bring into his disposable estate. And, at least one school of thought scorns any method of valuation which omits from the decision-making process the partners' own thoughts on the matter.

(5) VALUATION BY FORMULA. Increasingly, it seems, are businessmen turning to valuation by formula as a way to settle the price question. This can be identical to the book-value approach, but more often than not it is a combination of factors which make up the formula — the whole ball of wax being applied to the partnership when the first partner dies, either by an impartial outsider or by the surviving partners and the personal representative of the deceased. This way of setting price makes a great deal of sense. Accurate funding is made possible inasmuch as the formula can be applied at any moment in time. By the same token, a partner is permitted to know in advance reasonably well what his estate can expect to receive for his business interests. Moreover, the price obtained would, all other things being equal, hold for estate-tax purposes. And, there would be no

burden of periodic revaluations, as are essential in the agreed-dollar approach. Certainly, it would be desirable now and then to apply the formula to determine if the funding were still adequate, but, generally speaking, the "time-clock" obligation to do so would not be as pressing.

Just described above are five fairly different ways of handling the problem of valuation. There certainly are others. But, and this bears emphasis, there is *no magic* in any one or in any combination of them. No built-in guarantee of accuracy, of precise tailoring of the price which would *in theory* prevail in an ideal market. Perhaps the wisest step for partners who are faced with this problem to take is to retain the services of an accountant in whose ability and integrity each of them has confidence. Another way of saying this is that the fee charged by a competent accountant is well earned.

Now and then the question is raised, "Can a purchase agreement *among family members* establish valuation for estate-tax purposes, assuming inclusion of a properly drawn price provision?" A father, for example, may want to have his share of the business sold out upon death to his son, and the fear is that the Internal Revenue Service will view the sale at least in part as a gift transaction; that is, there is a real danger that the Internal Revenue Service will conclude that the transaction was *not* a so-called arm's-length agreement. Certainly it is true that intra-family buy-outs invite close scrutiny by the Service,* but it has been suggested that if the parties engage a reputable and impartial accountant to make the valuation, there is at least a better chance that the resulting price will be nailed down for estate-tax purposes.

It should be remembered that when a partner dies on a date other than the close of the tax year, *his* tax year closes† and he (his estate) is entitled to his distributive share of earnings to such date. Generally it is agreed that the determination and payment of such distributive share are something quite apart from valuation of and payment for his partnership interest.

RECEIVABLES, INVENTORY AND GOOD WILL. A discussion of valuation would be grossly incomplete if certain additional points were not at least raised. One has already been analyzed in the preceding

---

* See COMMISSIONER V. BENSEL, 100 F.2d 639 (C.A. 3, 1938); but see ESTATE OF BISCHOFF V. COMMISSIONER, 69 T.C. 32(1977) (upholding estate valuation determined by buy-sell agreement even though the other partners were the "natural objects of bounty" of the deceased partner).

† See Section 706(c)(2).

chapter — the problem of ballooning which is present whenever an entity-purchase plan is adopted. (See page 23 above.) Mention of three other items is made here simply to bring them into focus in the over-all picture of valuation, even though each is discussed in some detail in the following chapter on "Tax Considerations."

First, unrealized receivables* may or may not present a problem in an ordinary business-partnership purchase plan. Usually such an account does not form the major share of partnership assets as it might very likely in a professional or personal-service partnership. To the extent, however, that a partnership does have a substantial portion of unrealized receivables, such should be included in the over-all purchase price, and attention ought to be paid to the tax treatment of payments made for a partner's interest in them. Generally, payment for a partner's share of unrealized receivables is includible as ordinary income by the recipient and may, or may not, reduce the distributive shares of earnings to the remaining partners. Unrealized receivables also include the amount which would be treated as ordinary income if certain partnership property were sold for its fair market value; the property involved includes property subject to depreciation and accelerated cost recovery property (described in Code Sections 1245 and 1250), mining property (described in Code Section 617), certain farm land (described in Code Sections 1251 and 1252), stock in a DISC (described in Code Section 992), franchises, trademarks or trade names (described in Code Section 1253), and oil, gas or geothermal properties (described in Code Section 1254). The purpose of this provision is to "recapture" the tax benefit that was obtained through various deductions which, in general, exceeded the economic loss. Thus, to the extent that a partnership has substantial amounts of machinery or other equipment, or real property, that has been subject to heavy tax depreciation but which has not sustained the same amount of economic depreciation, the payment for a partner's interest in that property would be ordinary income.

Second, there exists an analogous problem with inventory, which is most often found in regular business partnerships and not in personal-service partnerships. If the fair market value of a partnership's inventory rises beyond a certain point and if such value

---

* Work in progress, rights to payment for goods delivered or to be delivered or services rendered or to be rendered.

exceeds a certain portion of all partnership property, then you have — in the words of the 1954 Internal Revenue Code — an inventory which has "appreciated substantially." If this be so, then, like payments for unrealized receivables, payments made for substantially appreciated inventory may be partly includible in ordinary income by the recipient.

Finally, what about good will? The tax status of payments for the good will of an ordinary business partnership appears to be clear. This is good news. But, it should be observed that by virtue of different characterizations of the payment for good will different tax effects can result both to the payor and to the recipient. And it certainly is important to a recipient of any such payment for good will if the amount received is includible in income or not.

A difference in the net (after-tax) value of a partner's interest in unrealized receivables, substantially appreciated inventory, or good will can be made to result by spreading out over more than one tax year what would otherwise be a lump-sum payment, or, in the case of good will, by designating the payments in the agreement as one thing or another. In short, the *manner* of payment as well as the *characterization* of the payment may affect valuation.

Tax Considerations

TAXES — the one denominator common to a colonial tea party, alphabetized government, illicit gin and epigastric distress. While such a definition is not to be found in any standard dictionary, it is probably true that most payors and non-payors of taxes would appreciate the logic. But, be that as it may, taxes are such a fact of life, and death, that a little volume such as this would be hopelessly wanting without some explanation of the tax implications of the business behavior suggest herein. How badly "hurt" or how "well off" will the person be who pays and the person who receives under a partnership-purchase plan? Are there any devices by which the taxpayer can be relieved of his misery, short of suicide?

The answers to these and other related questions can perhaps best be reached by engaging in a little basic analysis of the payments made:

(1) Is the payment made *by a partner* for a partner's interest *or* is the payment made *by the partnership?* This is the distinction between *a sale* and *a liquidation* of a partner's interest.

(2) Is the payment made to a partner or to his successor in interest? That is, is the partner whose interest is being sold or liquidated *alive* or *dead?*

(3) Is the payment made in *one lump sum* or is it *spread out*

over two or more years?

(4) If the payment is spread out, is it *fixed* in amount *or* is it *based upon partnership earnings?*

These are the major distinctions made by the 1954 Internal Revenue Code in "subchapter K — Partners and Partnerships." Keep these in mind, and you will have won half the battle. Keep in mind, as well, that "subchapter K" is quite complex; what follows is but an overview of the problems that the subchapter raises.

Before we plunge into the detailed questions which are commonly asked by participants in partnership-purchase plans, it might be wise to learn some of the "lingo" commonly employed in this area.

"INTEREST IN THE PARTNERSHIP." When tax people talk of payments made in liquidation of or for the sale of a partner's "interest in the partnership," they ordinarily mean that "interest in the partnership" is property which is subject to capital gain (or loss) treatment. Sometimes tax folks use a shorthand term instead, viz., "interest in capital assets." In contradistinction are the items discussed immediately below.

"UNREALIZED RECEIVABLES." Unrealized receivables include the partnership's rights to payment for goods or services, which rights have not been included in gross income under the method of accounting used by the partnership. While the term as so applied has little application in accrual-basis partnerships inasmuch as matured income items ordinarily will have been included in gross income, cash-basis partnerships usually have some assets which are properly labelled "unrealized receivables." The most common ledger entry in this connection is "accounts receivable," but there are others such as "notes receivable." And, in both accrual-basis and cash-basis partnerships there is often found an account entitled "work in progress" which is also an unrealized receivable.

Unrealized receivables also include the amount which would be treated as ordinary income if certain partnership property were sold for its fair market value; the kinds of property involved include property subject to depreciation (described in Code Sections 1245 and 1250), section 1245 recovery property, mining property (described in Code Secton 617), certain farm land (described in Code Sections 1251 and 1252), stock in a DISC (described in Code Section 992), franchises, trademarks, or trade names (described in Code Section 1253), and oil, gas, or geothermal properties (described in Code Section 1254). The purpose of this provision is to "recapture" the tax benefit that was obtained through varius deductions which, in general, exceeded the economic loss. Thus, to the extent that a partnership has substantial amounts of equipment, or real property, that has been subject to heavy tax depreciation, the payment for a partner's interest in that property would be ordinary income. The Internal Revenue Code, in Section 751, defines unrealized receivables as follows:

> (c) Unrealized Receivables — For purposes of this subchapter, the term "unrealized receivables" includes, to the extent not previously includable in income under the method of accounting used by the partnership, any rights (contractual or otherwise) to payment for —
>
> > (1) goods delivered, or to be delivered, to the extent the proceeds therefrom would be treated as amounts received from the sale or exchange of property other than a capital asset, or
> > (2) services rendered, or to be rendered.
>
> For purposes of this section an sections 731, 736, and 741, such term also includes mining property (as defined in section 617(f)(2), stock in a DISC (as described in section 992(a)), section 1245 property (as defined in section 1245(a)(3)), section 1245 property (as defined in section 1245(a)(5)), stock in certain foreign corporations (as described in section 1248), section 1250 property (as defined in section 1250(c)), farm recapture property (as defined in section 1251(e)(1)), farm land (as defined in section 1252(a)), franchises, trademarks or trade names (referred to in section 1253(a)), and an oil, gas or geothermal property (described in section 1254) but only to the extent of the amount which would be treated as capital gain to which section 617(d)(1), 995(c), 1245(a), 1248(a), 1250(a), 1251(c), 1252(a), 1253(a) or 1254(a) would apply if (at the time of the transaction described in this section or section 731, 736, or 741, as the case may be) such property had been sold by the partnership at its fair market value. For purposes of this section and sections 731, 736, and 741, such term also includes any market discount bond (as defined in section 1278) and any short-term obligation (as defined in section 1283) but only to the extent of the amount which would be treated as ordinary income if (at the time of the transaction described in this section or section 731, 736, or 741, as the case may be) such property had been sold by the partnership.

"SUBSTANTIALLY APPRECIATED INVENTORY." Business partnerships which deal in products have an "inventory" — assets held for ordinary business sales.* In the usual case inventory is simply stock in

---

* Technically, for purposes of the Code, inventory also includes other non-capital assets or non-Section 1231 assets, e.g., a copyright, a literary, artistic or musical composition, etc. See Section 751(d)(2).

trade, all the goods owned by the business which are held primarily for sale to customers. There are times when the inventory may rise in value from the time it was first "stacked on the shelves." The manufacturer's price, for example, could have risen, or a general inflationary spiral could have taken place. Section 751(d)(1) of the Code tells us that "[i]nventory items of the partnership shall be considered to have appreciated substantially in value if their fair market value exceeds (A) 120 percent of the adjusted basis to the partnership of such property, and (B) 10 percent of the fair market value of all partnership property, other than money." If inventory has appreciated in value, then the question arises as to what sort of tax treatment should be accorded to that portion of the partner's gain which is attributable to the inventory appreciation. The purpose behind the Code's specific categorization of substantially appreciated inventory is really quite simple: If the inventory has appreciated *substantially,* then that portion of the gain attributed to the selling partner is to be taxed as ordinary income. If, for example, the adjusted basis of the partnership's inventory is $2,000 and the current fair market value of such inventory is $3,000, and if the fair market value of all other partnership property (other than money), such as the building in which the business is carried on, is less than $27,000, then the inventory has appreciated substantially and there would be a potential gain to the partnership of $1,000, and in a buy-out situation that portion of the selling partner's gain which is attributable to the inventory appreciation could be taxed as ordinary income.

Now, let us turn to particular factual situations and see what happens tax-wise to the persons who pay and the persons who receive under the terms of a traditional partnership-purchase agreement.* And, in order that we can talk in "shorthand," A, B and C will be our partners, and C, poor C, if anyone is to die, will be our choice.

CROSS-PURCHASE PAYMENTS

For purposes of this discussion we can forget that entity-purchase plans exist. Here we shall see what happens when the remaining partners buy out another's partnership interest. Sales, not liquidations.

---

* We shall assume, throughout, that all of the partners and the partnership operate on a cash basis. In addition, we shall assume that all payments are made in money, not in kind.

Cross-Purchase Payments: To a Retiring Partner: Lump-Sum Payment.

If A and B buy C's partnership interest from him while he is alive, then a certain part of the payment that A makes to C and that B makes to C will be in consideration of C's "interest in the partnership." A and B, since they are purchasing capital assets, will receive no deduction, or reduction, in their distributive shares of the partnership earnings, and C (assuming no gain or loss) will report no income. To the extent, however, that a part of A's and B's payments represent consideration for C's interest in the unrealized receivables or substantially appreciated inventory, C will experience ordinary income. This makes sense because C is really anticipating future distributive shares of partnership income, including his proportionate share of its ordinary income resulting from the "recapture rules."

But, what about A and B? Do they enjoy a deduction, or do they have some sort of offset to relieve the income-tax burden, when the purchased receivables are realized and the substantially appreciated inventory they bought is ultimately sold? No. If that is so, then what on earth would ever possess A and B to get into such an arrangement where they would pay after-tax dollars for before-tax income items? Well, there is a reason and it is a good one: If the continuing partnership, directed by A and B, files an election under Section 754 of the 1954 Internal Revenue Code to adjust the basis of partnership property in the manner described in Section 743, relief is available. Section 743(b) indicates that:

> In the case of a transfer of an interest in a partnership by sale or exchange . . . a partnership . . . shall . . . increase the adjusted basis of the partnership property by the excess of the basis to the transferee partner of his interest in the partnership over his proportionate share of the adjusted basis of the partnership property . . . .

That Section further states that "such increase . . . shall constitute an adjustment to the basis of partnership property with respect to the transferee partner only." A and B in such a situation would be the "transferee" partners. Thus, for example, if C's share of the unrealized receivables and substantially appreciated inventory amounted to $5,000 and A and B, being equal partners, each paid C $2,500 for such interest, then, assuming the election is made, their basis in those income accounts would be increased. What does all this mean? Simply that, for instance, when some of the purchased receivables are realized by the partnership and when the distributive shares of A and B are computed, each of them will enjoy a reduction in his reportable distributive share corresponding to this increased basis in such receivables. Why? Because their basis in the receivables and substantially appreciated inventory would be "stepped up" by the amount each one paid for them. While technically it is *not* so, it is *as if* A and B each were allowed a deduction; A and B will experience ordinary income with respect to C's share of unrealized receivables and substantially appreciated inventory only to the extent that such unrealized receivables and substantially appreciated inventory "sugar off" for more than A and B paid for them. At this point a patient reader might venture, "That is a frightfully tortuous merry-go-round to accomplish something really quite simple — our tax laws could not be more devious!" Well, they certainly could be, and further, they do make sense especially when one contemplates a situation where D, a stranger to the partnership, buys C's interest.

Cross-Purchase Payments: To a Retiring Partner: Spread-Out Payments.

What happens when just one fact is changed in the situation presented above, i.e., the consideration paid to C is spread out over two or more years? Probably C would like a spread-out so that his income would not be accelerated and heaped together where it would suffer a needlessly high tax rate. A leveling of income to C would normally be wise from a tax standpoint. By postponing his income share, however, C does run the risk that A and B will not be able, during the period of such spread-out, to meet their obligations. The desirability to C of having A's and B's payments spread out may depend, in part, on the effect of the "income averaging" provisions of the Code. If C's income for the year in which A's and B's payments are received is disproportionately large as compared with his income for the prior three years (that is, if his adjusted taxable income for the year the payments are received exceeds 140% of his average income for the three prior years), then under Code Sections 1301–1305 the excess income is taxed at rates somewhat lower than would otherwise be the case.

From the viewpoint of A and B, it would appear that they also should favor such an arrangement because, as a practical matter, their financial obligations to C would be easier to fund. There would not be the one large lump-sum payment to raise right off the bat; conceivably, at least some part of their payments to C could be plucked from current distributive shares of partnership income. And, note that the election under Section 754 is a *continuing* one; thus, as each payment is made by A and B, their basis in the unrealized receivables and substantially appreciated inventory is correspondingly increased.

Cross-Purchase Payments: To a Deceased Partner's Successor in Interest: Lump-Sum Payment.

Now, let us get back to the lump-sum payment and kill off C. In such a case A and B would not be paying C, but C's executor or administrator. What happens income-tax-wise to C's personal representative? Prior to 1971 it had been suggested that A's and B's payments to C's personal representative would not result in any income for the reason that the partnership interest in the hands of C's personal representative had a basis equal to its date-of-death value and so would reflect the value of the unrealized receivables; when the receivables were collected, they would be offset by their basis. However, this view has been rejected on the ground that such receivables are income in respect of a decedent and, therefore, under Code Section 1014(c) are not to be accorded a basis reflecting their date-of-death value. WOODHALL V. COMMISSIONER, 454 F.2d 226 (9th Cir. 1972); QUICK'S TRUST V. COMMISSIONER, 444 F.2d 90 (8th Cir. 1971). The significance of the distinction between income in respect of a decedent and other property included in C's estate would have been decreased by the carry-over-basis rule (Section 1023) originally enacted as part of the Tax Reform Act of 1976. Those rules, however, were repealed by the Crude Oil Windfall Profit Tax Act of 1980.

The 1980 Act reinstated the rule of Section 1014 which provides that the basis of capital assets passing to C's estate (including C's partnership interest, excluding unrealized receivables) is equal to its value as of the date of C's death (or the alternate valuation date). Therefore, a sale of these assets to the remaining partners would not normally result in any taxable gain or loss. For example, A, B and C enter into a partnership on January 1, 1984 with all three making an initial capital investment of $10,000. Thereafter C dies on January 1, 1985. Immediately after C's death his partnership interest is worth $120,000 of which $30,000 is attributable to unrealized receivables. C's successor-in-interest then sells C's interest to the remaining partners for $120,000. Under the present law, the $30,000 attributable to unrealized receivables would be taxed as ordinary income, and the $90,000 attributable to the sale of the partner's interest in the partnership's other capital assets would pass tax free since the purchase price was traded "even Stephen" for the decedent's interest in the assets.

Cross-Purchase Payments: To a Deceased Partner's Successor in Interest: Spread-Out Payments.

Here we simply change one fact, viz., spread-out payments instead of a lump sum. Tax-wise there would be no difference from the conclusions reached immediately above. A spread-out would probably be advantageous to C's executor or administrator; an estate cannot income average. If the payments were made to C's wife as his successor in interest (rather than to this executor or administrator), the determination of whether a spread-out is beneficial would have to be made with consideration of income averaging.

One important fact bearing on whether the deceased partner's successor in interest would benefit from a spread-out is that the partnership taxable year does not close with respect to a deceased partner as it does where a partner's interest in the partnership is either sold or liquidated. Code Section 706(c). The effect of this provision is to require the deceased partner's successor in interest to report the deceased partner's distributive share of partnership income for the partnership year in which his date of death falls. Any amounts actually received by the deceased partner from the partnership prior to his death are not reported on his final return, and the deceased partner's final return, therefore, may show substantially more (personal) deductions than income. One method of avoiding this unfortunate result is to designate the surviving spouse as the successor in interest. Another is to have the estate make a distribution to the surviving spouse. Either method results in the deceased partner's distributive share of firm income being reported on his final joint return, and thus being offset by his personal deductions. In all probability the spread-out of payments is likely to produce a lower tax, particularly if the deceased partner's distributive share of partnership income for his final year of participation in the firm is reported by the same person who reports the amounts received for his partnership interest (including his share of unrealized receivables).

ENTITY-PURCHASE PAYMENTS

Now, let us think about those situations where the *partnership,* not the partners, makes the payments. This is the area of liquidations, not sales.

Entity-Purchase Payments: To a Retiring Partner: Lump-Sum Payment.

What are the tax consequences to the retiring partner when he receives a lump-sum payment for all of his interest in the partnership? The answer depends again upon the *nature* of the total interest being paid for. First, we can conclude that that portion of the distribution which can be attributed to his "interest in partnership property" will not be ordinary income to him* (although if there is capital gain or loss, it will be recognized). Neither will that part of the payment explicitly ear-marked in the buy-out agreement as the price for his share of the good will of the partnership,† although it would be subject to capital gains tax. If a payment in lieu of a payment for good will is made and the partnership agreement does *not* provide for a payment for good will, then that payment will be taxed to the retiring partner as ordinary income.** Payment for unrealized receivables will also be taxed as ordinary income.‡ And, so too with regard to payment for the retiring partner's interest in substantially appreciated inventory, although it is interesting to observe how roundabout the statute is in this regard: Section 751, which ostensibly deals with *sales,* not liquidations, states that certain distributions *by the partnership* shall "be considered as a sale," among them being money paid for substantially appreciated inventory.*** If there is any other payment than those mentioned immediately above, such as in connection with a so-called "mutual insurance" arrangement, it will be taxed as ordinary income.‡‡

How does all this affect the remaining partners? Payment for the interest in the partnership, which is not income to the retiring partner, does nothing helpful or harmful tax-wise to them, although if C

---

* Section 736(b)(1).

† Section 736(b)(2)(B).

** Section 736(a)(2).

‡ Section 736(b)(2)(A).

*** Section 751(b)(1). Income Tax Regulations Sections 1.736-1(b)(4) and 1.751-1(c)(4)(ii).

‡‡ Section 736(a).

experienced a gain and if the election under Section 754 were in effect, then the basis of the partnership's assets is stepped up for the remaining partners to the extent of the gain. Payment, however, for unrealized receivables and substantially appreciated inventory items which are reportable in the retiring partner's income does step up (without regard to the Section 754 election) the partnership's basis in those items with the result that the partnership reflects less reportable income. And, as to the items of income to the retiring partner under Section 736(a)(1) or (a)(2), payment by the partnership therefor is treated as a distribution to the retiring partner and therefore reduces the distributive shares tax-wise to the remaining partners.

Entity-Purchase Payments: To a Retiring Partner: Spread-Out Payments.

Only one fact is changed — instead of a lump-sum payment, it is decided to spread the payment over two or more years. The difference in tax consequences is clear; income to the retiring partner as well as reductions in distributive shares to the remaining partners and adjustment to bases for the partnership can be levelled so as to avoid the comparatively higher tax rates.

Spread-out is permitted by the Regulations appurtenant to Section 736, and moreover, there has been provided some flexibility. If, for example, the installments are fixed in amount, then an equal fixed portion of each payment will be deemed as a payment for an interest in capital assets, so-called, and the balance as an income payment.* If, on the other hand, the annual payment is tied to partnership earnings which are not fixed in amount, the first payments are to be deemed in exchange for the retiring partner's interest in partnership property and subsequent payments as income.† However, if such an allocation does not meet the parties' taste, they may provide for any other reasonable formula.**

It should be noted that it is also possible for the parties to agree for payments to be made to a retiring partner over a period certain or for his life. Such payments, which would be deductible by the partnership under Section 736(a)(1), would be in the nature of mutual

---

* Income Tax Regulations Sections 1.736-1(b)(5)(i).

† Income Tax Regulations Sections 1.736-1(b)(5)(ii).

** Income Tax Regulations Sections 1.736-1(b)(5)(iii).

insurance to provide a retiring partner with the equivalent of a non-qualified pension and could be used in conjunction with a qualified retirement plan (a so-called H.R. 10 Plan). Such payments would be in addition to payments for his interest in partnership property and would be taxable to the retiring partner as ordinary income when received.

Entity-Purchase Payments: To a Deceased Partner's Successor in Interest: Lump-Sum Payment.

Alas, C died before attaining retirement age, and now the partnership is obligated to pay his personal representative the price established by the partnership's entity-purchase agreement. Are there any tax consequences to C's personal representative different from those that would have resulted had C decided to retire instead of die? In this regard two points should be made.

First, the part of the payment which is attributable to income items and which would have been ordinary income to C if C had lived to retirement is still income to C's personal representative; Section 753 is explicit in stating the "[t]he amount includible in the gross income of a successor in interest of a deceased partner under section 736(a) shall be considered income in respect of a decedent under section 691." This means that such amount will retain its same income character in the hands of the recipient.* If the recipient must report such income, then he has available a deduction against such income for the estate tax paid with respect to it. Query, what about substantially appreciated inventory? Prior to the repeal of the carry-over basis rules enacted by the Tax Reform Act of 1976, C's portion of the gain in substantially appreciated inventory would have been taxed as ordinary income regardless of whether a basis adjusting election under Section 754 was made. Now, however C's personal representative will not have to include in income that part of the price paid for that portion of the gain attributable to C's interest in the partnership's substantially appreciated inventory if the partnership had made a basis-adjusting election under Section 754. Since the basis of the property in the hands of C's personal representative would have been computed immediately

---

* Section 691(a).

following the death of C, subsequent to the stepping up of the basis of the property under Section 754, no gain would have been recognized. Conversely, if the partnership had failed to make that election, the C's portion of the gain in substantially appreciated inventory would have been taxed as ordinary income, although there would have been an offsetting capital loss.

Second, C's personal representative now receives that portion of the payment attributable to his interest in partnership property free of any capital gain, because the estate's basis for C's interest in partnership property will be the value of C's interest upon his death as established by the buy-sell agreement.*

It would appear that as far as the surviving partners are concerned the tax consequences to them would be identical to those mentioned above in the discussion dealing with a lump-sum payment by the partnership to a *retiring* partner.

Entity-Purchase Payments: To a Deceased Partner's Successor in Interest: Spread-Out Payments.

The only difference here is that the partnership spreads out its payments to C's personal representative instead of making one lump-sum payment. And, the tax consequences are identical with only one exception — income to C's estate is deferred into presumably lower tax brackets. The partnership's ability to "deduct" its income payment is correspondingly deferred.

Actually a spread out of payments may be especially desirable if each partner is willing to gamble that the partnership's ability to pay will remain in good shape during the period of such installments. The reason is that, as a practical matter, it often happens that the net partnership income does not drop a full proportionate share when one of the partners dies. What usually transpires is that the survivors have to work a little harder to keep up with most of the business, and for the partnership's obligation to buy out the deceased's share the remaining partners would show substantially higher income. Thus, if such circumstances can be predicted with reasonable certainty, it would obviously be wise to agree to a spread-out.

---

* See "Valuation" herein at page 30.

GOOD WILL

The Internal Revenue Service has conceded that a professional practice can have saleable good will. Revenue Ruling 70-45, 1970-1 C.B.
17. But in the case of a business partnership the basis for the Internal
Revenue Service's challenge to the existence of good will in a professional practice, that is, that good will could not exist because the
business was wholly dependent upon professional skill or other personal
characteristics of the owner, did not obtain. On a sale of a partnership
interest (a cross-purchase situation) payment made for good will will be
accorded capital gain treatment to the seller, but that payment will be
non-deductible by the new partner. Similarly, where payment is made
by the partnership for a partner's interest therein, the amount which is
paid for good will will be accorded capital gain treatment, under Section 736(b)(2)(B), to the extent that the partnership agreement provides for a good-will payment, but the amount so paid will not be
deductible by the partnership; to the extent the partnership agreement
does not provide for a good-will payment, the payment is ordinary income to the recipient and deductible by the partnership under Section
736(a).

THE FUNDING INSURANCE

Premium payments — are they deductible?

Whether the premiums are paid by the partnership under an
entity plan or by a partner under a cross-purchase plan, such payments
are *not* deductible. Regulation Section 1.264-1 makes this clear:

> (a) When premiums are not deductible. Premiums paid by a tax-
> payer on a life insurance policy are not deductible from the
> taxpayer's gross income, even though they would otherwise be deduc-
> tible as trade or business expenses, if they are paid on a life insurance
> policy covering the life of any officer or employee of the taxpayer, or
> any person (including the taxpayer) who is financially interested in
> any trade or business carried on by the taxpayer, when the taxpayer
> is directly or indirectly the beneficiary of the policy.

This should neither shock nor dismay the reader. After all, the use of
insurance is only one, albeit demonstrably the best, type of funding
vehicle. The potential purchaser could instead bury his money or in-
vest it in antique pewter. Thus, non-deductibility of premium

payments should not be viewed gloomily, any more than one should be justifiably unhappy over the fact that savings bank deposits are not deductible for income-tax purposes.

Premium payments by the partnership — are they includible in income to the partners?

Under an entity-purchase plan, it should be obvious that premium payments by the partnership for insurance owned by and payable to it are not income to the individual partners. The partnership is simply carrying an asset in one form (life insurance) instead of another (cash, securities, etc.). However, it is important to bear in mind that to the extent premium payments are made out of partnership earnings they do not reduce the distributive shares of income to the partners. This fact can be significant and is perhaps best illustrated by an example. A is 55 years old and his two partners are 30 and 35, respectively. Their entity-purchase agreement omits the value (either cash surrender value or face proceeds) of the funding insurance from the valuation or price provision. Observe how, as a practical matter, A must pay income tax each year on his total distributive share of partnership earnings, which share has not been reduced by the premiums paid for the insurance on his life, or for the insurance on the others either. Is not A, at least in part, buying himself out — and with after-tax dollars? The burden on A in such a case can be at least partially avoided by including in the purchase price some provision for the funding insurance as an asset of the partnership.

Policy proceeds — are they taxable as income to the recipient policyowner?

The answer to this particular question spotlights one of the real clinchers militating in favor of using life insurance as the funding vehicle. The proceeds, whether received by the partnership involved in an entity-purchase plan or by co-partners under a cross-purchase arrangement, arrive income-tax free when paid to the owner of the policy. Section 101(a) of the 1954 Internal Revenue Code states that "gross income does not include amounts received (whether in a single sum or otherwise) under a life insurance contract, if such amounts are paid by reason of the death of the insured." It should be pointed out, though, that if the proceeds are paid to the deceased partner's successor in interest *directly,* then they do not escape income taxation by virtue of the above-numbered section. In such a case the insurer is deemed to have made payment on behalf of or as agent of the policyowner.* It should be reemphasized, however, that it is unusual, as well as generally undesirable, to designate the insured's estate as beneficiary of partnership-owned or co-partner-owned life insurance used to fund buy-out agreements.†

Although this particular point should be self-evident, it should be noted that any disability-income payments made under any of the disability insurance does not receive the same protection as death proceeds — Section 101(a) refers only to payments made "by reason of the death of the insured." Whether such disability-income payments are received by the policyowner free of income taxation appears to be a question the answer to which is in some doubt.

Policy proceeds — are they includible in the estate of the insured when paid directly to his estate?

If the formula clause establishing the buy-out price is binding, not *both* the partnership interest and the insurance proceeds, if such proceeds are paid directly to the deceased's successor in interest, are includible for estate-tax purposes although the Commissioner might argue for such double inclusion.** Ordinarily the policy proceeds will be made payable to the policyowner and the policyowner will pay the purchase price as set out in the agreement to the estate of the deceased partner; and in such event the proceeds are not includible in the deceased insured's estate, although the value of his interest in the partnership is.‡‡

PURCHASE UPON DISABILITY

Some particular mention, perhaps, should be made regarding those buy-out agreements which provide for purchase or liquidation of a

---

* See Income Tax Regulations Sections 1.753-1(a).

† See discussion beginning at p. 28.

** See ESTATE OF TOMPKINS V. COMMISSIONER, 13 T.C. 1054 (1949); ESTATE OF WEIL V. COMMISSIONER, 22 T.C. 1267 (1954).

‡‡ ESTATE OF KNIPP V. COMMISSIONER, 25 T.C. 24 (1955), aff'd on other grounds, 244 F.2d 436 (4th Cir. 1957).

disabled partner's share in the partnership. Actually, there is nothing fearful in this area — the buy-out would be marked by the distinctions originally set out at the beginning of this chapter, e.g., payments either by the partnership or by the partners, to a partner and not to his successor-in-interest, and payment, almost undoubtedly, spread out rather than in a lump sum. It is, however, important to observe that (1) the payments would *not* be "sick pay" to the disabled partner (upon which there would be no income tax within certain limits) and (2) the "disability-income payments" made by the insurer to the partnership (in the case of entity funding) or to a co-partner (in the case of cross-purchase funding) *may be* income to the recipient. Another way of stating this is simply to say that the fact that the retiring partner is disabled may be irrelevant from a tax standpoint. And, finally, from a non-tax standpoint it should be emphasized that such payments to a disabled retiring partner should *not* be viewed as disability-income payments or payments in lieu thereof — the payments are made in exchange for or in liquidation of his partnership interest and should not dissuade him from providing, somehow, for himself the disability-income protection that every person needs in one form or another.

Use of
a Trustee

IN CONSIDERING THE ESTABLISHMENT of a partnership-purchase plan the prospective parties may face the question of whether or not a trustee should be used. And perhaps the best way to determine the answer to this question is to ask another: What needs can be satisfied by a trustee?

Perhaps the most widely experienced and important need to be served by a trustee in a business-purchase agreement is the parties' desire for an escrow. That is, it is oftentimes more comforting to all concerned to know that the plan will be administered by an impartial stranger to the buy-out contract. In this type of arrangement the trustee would be designated beneficiary of the funding policies whether for a cross-purchase or an entity-type plan and would hold the proceeds in much the same manner as does a title company when it acts as escrow in a land-purchase transaction. Sometimes it is known, before the death of a partner, that some suspicion, jealousy or ill will might arise among the surviving partners and the heirs or personal representative of a deceased partner. Certainly in such situations the need for some impartial administration is clear. Query, however, whether a trustee is the desirable agent to satisfy this need.

A particular danger spot in using a trustee exists where the purchase agreement provides for spread-out income payments taxable as such to the retiring partner or to the deceased partner's successor in interest. In a professional or personal-service partnership the lion's share of all payments to a deceased partner's estate may be of this income type; only in the non-personal-service partnership does one ordinarily find property not subject to ordinary income taxation in larger proportions.

If the right created by the purchase agreement to receive fixed-amount income payments is nonforfeitably vested in the retiring partner or in the deceased partner's designee and if also the promise in the purchase agreement is funded by designating the trustee as beneficiary of the insurance policy, then the situation is perilously close to the central problems of "constructive receipt" and "economic benefit" found in non-qualified deferred compensation or pension plans. The doctrine of "constructive receipt" is quite thoroughly discussed in Revenue Ruling 60-31, 1960-1 C.B. 174; the doctrine of "economic benefit" (or "cash equivalence") is discussed in SPROULL V. COMMISSIONER, 16 T.C. 244 (1951), aff'd, 194 F.2d 541 (C.A. 6, 1952). It would seem that if (1) the retiring partner or the deceased partner's successor in interest has a nonforfeitable vested right to receive the income installments, (2) the income installment payments are fixed in amount and (3) the trustee as beneficiary of the funding insurance receives proceeds sufficient to satisfy the purchase-contract income payments, then the doctrine of constructive receipt would apply. If it did apply, then the present value of all annual income payments would be income to the recipient in the first year, thus causing a lumping together of income and a probable consequent jump into a higher income-tax bracket, subject to the mitigating effect of the income averaging provisions of the Code. If some or all of the income payments are not guaranteed *fixed* amounts but are based instead upon a proportion or a percentage of the partnership's profits, then one might successfully argue that while the right to receive the income payments is vested, it is at the same time forfeitable. After all, the expected profits could turn out to be losses. In such event, however, there may still be a danger from the doctrine of economic benefit. If fixed amounts are not used, and if the Internal Revenue Service argues constructive receipt or economic benefit, how can it commute the value of such uncertain future amounts so that the taxpayer will have a reasonably certain present value upon which he can be expected to pay his tax?

In view of the discussion immediately above, it may be wise to avoid the use of a trustee in partnership-purchase plans where the income installments are fixed in amount, and perhaps even where such income installments are based upon the partnership's future profits.

Some use has been made of a trustee in *cross-purchase* cases (1) where the number of partners involved would otherwise cause the number of funding policies to become unwieldy or (2) where quantity discount premium rates would otherwise be available. In these situations the parties have agreed to a classic cross-purchase arrangement with a trustee *except* that the trustee is also made policyowner and premium payor. Care should be taken in the agreement to spell out clearly for whom the trustee holds the policy. For example, no ownership, legal or beneficial, in a policy should be attributable to the insured; if this is overlooked, then there is a possibility that maturing insurance would be held to be includible in the deceased partner's (the insured's) estate, a consequence obviously undesirable. In addition, counsel for the parties should want to make absolutely certain that the danger of constructive receipt of income as discussed above is avoided.

Specimen Agreements

THE SPECIMEN AGREEMENTS which follow are included for the convenience of the lawyer who is retained to draft the partnership-purchase plan. As was pointed out in the Preface, these are offered as examples only, something against which the attorney can measure the instrument he prepares to fit the precise facts of his case and the desires of his client. The drafting of such a buy-out agreement is the "practice of law" and is, therefore, a function wholly improper for the life underwriter, accountant or trust officer to assume. In this regard, it is perhaps worthwhile to mention that each party engaged in the task of business and estate planning should appreciate the proper limitations on the scope of his or her contributions to the over-all job.

No attempt has been made to include all of the formalities of execution which may be required in a particular jurisdiction. Further, we have left it up to counsel to decide whether, in the state in question, the spouse of a partner should join in the execution of the purchase agreement, as well as to judge the desirability of obligating each partner to have his will conform to the buy-out plan.

We have included specimen agreements "with trustee" even though there may be a substantial hazard in using a trustee; in this regard consult the chapter entitled "Use of a Trustee." The facts of a particular case may indicate that the income payments do not amount to very much, and, consequently, the acceleration of such payment for income-tax purposes might make little difference.

Specimen Business-Partnership Entity-
Purchase Agreement — Disability
Provisions — Without Trustee

AGREEMENT made this .... day of ...., 19........, by and between ...., ... and .... (hereinafter called "partners") and ...., (hereinafter called "the partnership").

WITNESSETH:

WHEREAS ...., ... and .... are co-partners in the business of ...., and

WHEREAS the interest of each partner in the partnership is as follows:

.... · · · · ....%
.... · · · · ....%
.... · · · · ....%

WHEREAS the primary purpose of this agreement is (1) to provide for the purchase by the partnership of the interest of any partner in the partnership in the event of the death or disability of a partner, (2) to provide for the purchase by the partners of the interest of a partner withdrawing from the partnership during his lifetime, (3) to provide further for the uninterrupted continuance of the partnership business upon the death or disability of a partner, and (4) to provide the funds necessary to carry out such purchase and sale,

NOW, THEREFORE, in consideration of the mutual agreements and covenants contained herein and for other valuable consideration, receipt of which is hereby acknowledged, it is mutually agreed and covenanted by the partners, each for himself, his heirs, assigns and personal representatives, and by the partnership, for itself as an entity, its successors and assigns, as follows:

Article 1. No partner shall during his lifetime assign, encumber or otherwise dispose of his interest or any part thereof in the partnership, except as provided below:

(1) If a partner should desire to dispose voluntarily of his interest during his lifetime, then he shall first offer in writing to sell his interest to the partnership at the price determined in accordance with the provisions of Article 2 below, provided, however, that such price shall be paid in cash, fully on the date of sale, and that the selling partner shall not participate in future profits of the partnership. If the interest is not purchased by the partnership within .... days of the receipt of the offer to it, then the selling partner may sell it to any other person but shall not sell it without first offering it to the partnership in accordance with the method established above at the price and on the terms offered to such other person if the price is less than the price established by Article 2. If, however, the partnership agreement forming this partnership further restricts, limits or prevents a lifetime sale or transfer by a partner of his interest in the partnership, then such partnership agreement shall prevail notwithstanding the provisions of this Article.

(2) In the event a partner party to this agreement becomes totally and permanently disabled before reaching age 55,* and remains so for a period of .... months† from the onset of such disability, then the partnership shall** purchase and the disabled partner shall sell, as of the end of such period, such disabled partner's interest in the partnership. "Disability" or "total and permanent disability" for purposes of this agreement shall be considered that disability of a particular insured partner which is described and determined by the insurer as total and permanent disability in the insurance policies on such insured partner listed in Article 3 below and/or Schedule B attached hereto, provided, however, that no insurer shall be subject to any liability other than its obligations in its policies of insurance. The purchase price shall be that which is established in Article 2 below, provided, however, that such purchase price shall not be paid in a lump sum but instead

---

* The cut-off age or date should be tied to the limitation, if any, in the funding vehicle.

† This period should be at least as long as the waiting period in the funding insurance, and probably longer.

** This language is mandatory in effect; sometimes an option to purchase is desired by the parties.

shall be paid in installments of $............. per month until the total purchase price shall have been paid plus an amount equal to .... % per year of the declining balance of such purchase price. If a disabled partner ceases to be so totally and permanently disabled at some time after such installment payments have commenced but before they have been completed, then* such installments shall be spread out further, namely, at the rate $............. per month until the balance of said purchase price and interest on the declining balance at the rate of .... % per year shall be wholly paid and satisfied.

Alternative Article 2. (This Article contemplates a payment in lieu of good will as an income item, *not* as a payment for good will as mentioned in Section 736(b)(2)(B) of the 1954 Internal Revenue Code. This Article contemplates the payment in lieu of good will to be treated as an income payment under Section 736(a) of the 1954 Internal Revenue Code.) Upon the death or disability of a partner, the partnership shall purchase and the estate of the deceased partner or the disabled partner shall sell his entire interest in the partnership for a price as determined below. It is agreed that the current fair value of the partnership's capital assets, as defined in Section 736(b) of the 1954 Internal Revenue Code, excluding good will, is $............., that the fair value of the accounts receivable, whether billed or unbilled, is $............., that the fair market value of the inventory is $............. and that, therefore, the value of each partner's interest† is as follows:

.... $.............
.... $.............
.... $.............

The partners agree to redetermine these values within .... days following the end of each (fiscal) (calendar) year, such redetermined values to be endorsed on Schedule A attached hereto and made a part of this agreement. If the partners fail to make such a redetermination

---

* This is simply one alternative; the parties could agree to stop the buy-out at such point, or they could even agree to let the disabled partner buy back in again.

† In the interest of simplicity we have assumed no outstanding liabilities of consequence. As a practical matter, however, where liabilities exist an adjustment for them should be made. One should remember that it is important to separate the values of capital and non-capital assets because if the determination is reasonable the Internal Revenue Service is inclined to accept it.

of values for a particular year, the last previously stipulated values shall control, except that if the partners fail to make such a determination within the .... months immediately preceding the death or onset of disability of a partner, then the values shall be agreed upon by the personal representative of the deceased partner or by the disabled partner on the one hand and the remaining partners on behalf of the partnership on the other. If they do not agree to a valuation within .... days after the death or onset of disability of the partner, the value of the deceased or disabled partner's interest shall be determined by arbitration as follows: The remaining partners on behalf of the partnership on the one hand and the representative of the deceased partner or the disabled partner on the other shall each name one arbitrator; if the two arbitrators cannot agree upon the values, then the two arbitrators shall appoint a third arbitrator and the decision of the majority shall be binding upon all parties. In determining values by arbitration, the arbitrators (must) (must not) take into account (the value of the life insurance proceeds accruing from the policies on the deceased partner's life) (the cash surrender value of the life insurance policies on the disabled partner's life).

The parties hereto agree and covenant that upon the death or disability of a partner the remaining partners shall continue the partnership business without interruption. Payment of the total purchase price as determined above shall be made with respect to a deceased partner's interest in the partnership in .... equal annual installments, the first such payment to be made within .... months from the date of the decedent partner's death, the intent of the parties being that the first payments shall represent payment for the capital assets (Section 736(b) payments), the latter payments for the balance. Payment of the total purchase price as determined above shall be made with respect to a disabled partner's interest in the partnership in accordance with the provisions of Article 1 above.

Upon the death or disability of a partner, the surviving partners shall continue the partnership business without interruption and the estate of the deceased partner or the disabled partner, as the case may be, shall participate in the net profits of the partnership business starting on the first day of the month following the date of his death or the onset of his disability and continuing for a period of .... years; the particular share shall equal to ....% of the net profits of the partnership as determined by the partnership's regular accountants. This additional payment has been agreed upon by the partners to represent a payment under and in accordance with Section 736(a)(1) of the 1954 Internal Revenue Code.*

Alternative Article 2. (This provision contemplates payment for good will as a capital asset or "interest in the partnership" in accordance with Section 736(b)(2)(B) of the 1954 Internal Revenue Code, *not* as an income payment under Section 736(a)(2) of the 1954 Internal Revenue Code.) Upon the death or disability of a partner, the partnership shall purchase and the estate of the deceased partner or disabled partner shall sell his entire interest in the partnership for a price as determined below. It is agreed that the current fair value of the partnership's capital assets as defined in Section 736(b) of the 1954 Internal Revenue Code, including good will, is $............, and that the fair market value of the inventory is $............ and that, therefore, the value of each partner's interest† is as follows:

-- · · · · $------------
-- · · · · $------------
-- · · · · $------------

The partners agree to redetermine these values within .... days following the end of each (fiscal) (calendar) year, such redetermined values to be endorsed on Schedule A attached hereto and made a part of this agreement. If the partners fail to make such a redetermination of values for a particular year, the last previously stipulated values shall control, except that if the partners fail to make such a redetermination within the .... months immediately preceding the death or onset of disability of a partner, then the values shall be agreed upon by the personal representative of the deceased partner or the disabled partner on the one hand and the remaining partners on behalf of the partnership on the other. If they do not agree to a valuation within .... days after the death or onset of disability of the partner, the value of the deceased or disabled partner's interest shall be determined by arbitration as follows: The remaining partners on behalf of the partnership on the one hand and the representative of the deceased partner or the disabled partner on the other shall each name one arbitrator; if the two arbitrators cannot agree upon the values, then the two arbitrators shall appoint a third arbitrator and the decision of the majority shall

---

* The paragraph provides for payment in lieu of good will as an income item.

† See second footnote on page 60.

be binding upon all parties. In determining values by arbitration, (the life insurance proceeds accruing from the policies on the deceased partner's life) (the cash surrender value of the policies of insurance on the life of the disabled partner) (must) (must not) be taken into account; further, an amount for the addition to the good will of the partnership by the deceased or disabled partner of not less than $............ shall be used.

The parties hereto agree and covenant that upon the death or disability of a partner the remaining partners shall continue the partnership business without interruption. Payment of the total purchase price as determined above shall be made with respect to a deceased partner's interest in the partnership in .... equal annual installments, the first such payment to be made .... months from the date of the decedent partner's death. Payment of the total purchase price as determined above shall be made with respect to a disabled partner's interest in the partnership in accordance with the provisions in Article 1 above.

Article 3. The partnership is the applicant, owner and beneficiary of the following life insurance policies issued by National Life Insurance Company:

> Policy #...........insuring the life of ----------------------------
> in the amount of $..............
>
> Policy #...........insuring the life of ----------------------------
> in the amount of $..............
>
> Policy #...........insuring the life of ----------------------------
> in the amount of $..............

In addition the partnership is the applicant, owner and beneficiary of the following disability income policies issued by National Life Insurance Company:

> Policy #...........on the life of ----------------------------
> in the amount of $..............
>
> Policy #...........on the life of ----------------------------
> in the amount of $..............
>
> Policy #...........on the life of ----------------------------
> in the amount of $..............

The partnership agrees to pay all premiums on the insurance policies taken out pursuant to this agreement and shall give proof of payment of premiums to the partners whenever any one of them shall so request such proof. If a premium is not paid within 20 days after its due date, the insured shall have the right to pay such premium and be reimbursed therefor by the partnership. The partnership shall have the right to purchase additional insurance on any of the partners; such additional policies shall be listed in Schedule B attached hereto and made a part of this agreement, along with any substitution or withdrawal of insurance policies subject to this agreement. In the event that the partnership decides to purchase additional insurance, each partner hereby agrees to co-operate fully by performing all the requisites of the insurer which are necessary conditions precedent to the issuance of insurance policies. Payment of premiums by the partnership shall be accounted for as an ordinary business expense.*

Article 4. Upon the death or disability of a partner the partnership shall pay the purchase price and make the payments as established by this agreement. The executor or administrator of the estate of the deceased partner or the disabled partner shall execute a bill of sale of his interest in the partnership to the partnership and a waiver of any right of accounting. At the same time the remaining partners shall execute and deliver to the estate of the deceased partner or to the disabled partner an agreement indemnifying the estate of the deceased partner or the disabled partner against all liabilities of the partnership. With respect to a deceased's interest in the partnership, the sale shall take effect as of the close of business on the day of death of the deceased partner and the unpaid balance of the purchase price, except for participation, if any, in profits, shall be evidenced by a series of promissory notes made by the surviving partners on behalf of the partnership to the order of the estate of the deceased; these notes shall provide for the acceleration of the due date of all unpaid notes in default in the payment of any note.

Article 5. Any partner who disposes of his interest in the partnership during his lifetime shall have the right to purchase the policy or policies of insurance on him owned by the partnership or by the other partners by paying an amount equal to the interpolated terminal reserve, if any, as of the date of transfer, plus the proportionate part of the gross premium last paid before the date of transfer which covers

---

* Not deductible; see page 50.

the period extending beyond that date, less any existing indebtedness charged against the policy or policies. This right shall lapse if not exercised within .... days after such disposal.

Article 6. The partners, the partnership and the personal representative of any deceased partner shall make, execute and deliver any documents necessary or desirable to carry out this agreement.

Article 7. This agreement may be altered, amended or terminated by a writing signed by all of the partners. In the event of a termination of this agreement before the death or disability of a partner, each partner shall be entitled to purchase from the partnership the policy or policies on him upon payment of an amount equal to the interpolated terminal reserve, if any, as of the date of transfer, plus the proportionate part of the gross premium last paid before the date of transfer which covers the period extending beyond that date, less any existing indebtedness charged against the policies.

Article 8. This agreement shall terminate upon the occurance of any of the following events:
(a) Bankruptcy of any partner,
(b) Bankruptcy, receivership or dissolution of the partnership, or
(c) Cessation of the partnership business.
In addition, this agreement shall be null and void if all the partners party hereto die within a period of 30 days.*

Article 9. Notwithstanding the provisions of this agreement, any insurance company whose policies are listed herein or in Schedule

---

* Counsel may feel that it would be desirable to treat simultaneous or rapidly suc cessive deaths differently. The close deaths of even two of the three partners raise problems. Let us take an example. If *A* and *B* die simultaneously, then under the entity agreement *C* ends up with ownership of the entire partnership. If the partnership was worth $90,000 while all were alive and the agreement was *fully* funded ($45,000 of insurance on each life), then *A*'s and *B*'s estates, assuming all were equal partners, would each receive $45,000. But because of ballooning (see discussion at page 23 above), i.e., maturation of *two* partnership-owned policies, the value of the partnership upon *two* deaths would be $180,000. One-third of $180,000 is $60,000, quite a substantial difference from the one-third value ($45,000) of the partnership if only one partner had died ($135,000). If *A* and *B* do not die simultaneously but rather *B* dies a few moments later, then the problem is similar although the inequity is limited to *B*'s estate only.

B attached is hereby authorized to act in accordance with the terms of any policies issued by it as if this agreement did not exist, and payment or other performance of its contractual obligations by the insurer in accordance with the terms of any such policies shall completely discharge the insurer from all claims and demands of all persons whomsoever. Any insurer is further authorized to provide to an insured partner any information with respect to the policy or policies on him owned by the partnership or by the other partners. No insurer shall be deemed or considered to be a party to this agreement for any purpose.

Article 10. Except as otherwise expressly stated herein, the partnership agreement heretofore existing among the parties is hereby amended by this agreement the provisions of which shall control. This agreement shall be governed by the law of the State of ....

IN WITNESS WHEREOF the parties hereto have executed this agreement at ...., in the County of ...., State of ...., on the day and the year above written.

-------------------------------------   ---------------------------------------

                                            By ----------------------------------

-------------------------------------   ---------------------------------------

-------------------------------------   ---------------------------------------

-------------------------------------   ---------------------------------------

Specimen Business-Partnership Entity-
Purchase Agreement — Disability
Provisions — With Trustee

AGREEMENT made this .... day of ....,
19........, by and between ...., ... and
.... (hereinafter called "partners"), ...,
(hereinafter called "the partnership"), and .... Trust
Company, a .... corporation (hereinafter called "Trustee").

WITNESSETH:

WHEREAS ....,
.... and ....,
are co-partners in the professional practice of ....,
............................., and

WHEREAS the interest of each partner in the partnership is as
follows:

.... · · · · ....%
.... · · · · ....%
.... · · · · ....%

WHEREAS the primary purpose of this agreement is (1) to provide for the purchase by the partnership of the interest of any partner in the partnership in the event of the death or disability of a partner, (2) to provide for the purchase by the partnership of the interest of a partner withdrawing from the partnership during his lifetime, (3) to provide further for the uninterrupted continuance of the partnership business upon the death or disability of a partner, and (4) to provide the funds necessary to carry out such purchase and sale,

NOW, THEREFORE, in consideration of the mutual agreements and covenants contained herein and for other valuable consideration, receipt of which is hereby acknowledged, it is mutually agreed and covenanted by the partners, each for himself, his heirs, assigns and personal representatives, and by the partnership, for itself as an entity, its successors and assigns, as follows:

Article 1. No partner shall during his lifetime assign, encumber or otherwise dispose of his interest or any part thereof in the partnership, except as provided below:

(1) If a partner should desire to dispose of his interest during his lifetime, then he shall first offer in writing to sell his interest to the partnership at the price determined in accordance with the provisions of Article 2 below, provided, however, that such price shall be paid in cash, fully on the date of sale, and that the selling partner shall not participate in future profits of the partnership. If the interest is not purchased by the partnership within .... days of the receipt of the offer to it, then the selling partner may sell it to any other person but shall not sell it without first offering it to the partnership in accordance with the method established above at the price and on the terms offered to such other person if the price is less than the price established by Article 2. If, however the partnership agreement forming this partnership further restricts, limits or prevents a lifetime sale or transfer by a partner of his interest in the partnership, then such partnership agreement shall prevail notwithstanding the provisions of this Article.

(2) In the event a partner party to this agreement becomes totally and permanently disabled before reaching age 55,* and remains so for a period of .... months† from the onset of such disability, then the partnership shall** purchase and the disabled partner shall sell, as of the end of such period, such disabled partner's interest in the partnership. "Disability" or "total and permanent disability" for purposes of this agreement shall be considered that disability of a particular insured partner which is described and determined by the insurer as total and permanent disability in the insurance policies on such insured partner listed in Article 3 below and/or Schedule B attached hereto, provided, however, that no insurer shall be subject to any liability other than its obligations in its policies of insurance. The purchase price shall be that which is established in Article 2 below, provided, however, that such purchase price shall not be paid in a lump sum but instead

---

* The cut-off age or date should be tied to the limitation, if any, in the funding vehicle.

† This period should be at least as long as the waiting period in the funding insurance, and probably longer.

** This language is mandatory in effect; sometimes an option to purchase is desired by the parties.

shall be paid in installments of $------------ per month until the total purchase price shall have been paid plus an amount equal to --------% per year of the declining balance of such purchase price. If a disabled partner ceases to be so totally and permanently disabled at some time after such installment payments have commenced but before they have been completed, then* such installments shall be spread out further, namely, at the rate of $------------ per month until the balance of said purchase price and interest on the declining balance at the rate of --------% per year shall be wholly paid and satisfied.

Alternative Article 2. (This Article contemplates a payment in lieu of good will as an income item, *not* as a payment for good will as mentioned in Section 736(b)(2)(B) of the 1954 Internal Revenue Code. This Article contemplates the payment in lieu of good will to be treated as an income payment under Section 736(a) of the 1954 Internal Revenue Code.) Upon the death or disability of a partner, the partnership shall purchase and the estate of the deceased partner or the disabled partner shall sell his entire interest in the partnership for a price as determined below. It is agreed that the current fair value of the partnership's capital assets, as defined in Section 736(b) of the 1954 Internal Revenue Code, excluding good will, is $------------, that the fair value of the accounts receivable, whether billed or unbilled, is $------------, that the fair market value of the inventory is $------------ and that, therefore, the value of each partner's interest† is as follows:

--- · · · · $------------
--- · · · · $------------
--- · · · · $------------

The partners agree to redetermine these values within --------days following the end of each (fiscal) (calendar) year, such redetermined values to be endorsed on Schedule A attached hereto and made a part of this agreement. If the partners fail to make such a redeter-

---

* This is simply one alternative; the parties could agree to stop the buy-out at such point, or they could even agree to let the disabled partner buy back in again.

† In the interest of simplicity we have assumed no outstanding liabilities of consequence. As a practical matter, however, where liabilities exist an adjustment for them should be made. One should remember that it is important to separate the values of capital and non-capital assets because if the determination is reasonable the Internal Revenue Service is inclined to accept it.

mination of values for a particular year, the last previously stipulated values shall control, except that if the partners fail to make such a redetermination within the .... months immediately preceding the death or onset of disability of a partner, then the values shall be agreed upon by the personal representative of the deceased partner or by the disabled partner on the one hand and the remaining partners on behalf of the partnership on the other. If they do not agree to a valuation within .... days after the death or onset of disability of the partner, the value of the deceased or disabled partner's interest shall be determined by arbitration as follows: The remaining partners on behalf of the partnership on the one hand and the representative of the deceased partner or the disabled partner on the other shall each name one arbitrator; if the two arbitrators cannot agree upon the values, then the two arbitrators shall appoint a third arbitrator and the decision of the majority shall be binding upon all parties. In determining values by arbitration, the arbitrators (must) (must not) take into account (the value of the life insurance proceeds accruing from the policies on the deceased partner's life) (the cash surrender value of the life insurance policies on the disabled partner's life).

The parties hereto agree and covenant that upon the death or disability of a partner the remaining partners shall continue the partnership business without interruption. Payment of the total purchase price as determined above shall be made with respect to a deceased partner's interest in the partnership in .... equal annual installments, the first such payment to be made within .... months from the date of the decedent partner's death, the intent of the parties being that the first payments shall represent payment for the capital assets (Section 736(b) payments), the latter payments for the balance. Payment of the total purchase price as determined above shall be made with respect to a disabled partner's interest in the partnership in accordance with the provisions of Article 1 above.

Upon the death or disability of a partner, the surviving partners shall continue the partnership business without interruption and the estate of the deceased partner or the disabled partner, as the case may be, shall participate in the net profits of the partnership business starting on the first day of the month following the date of his death or the onset of his disability and continuing for a period of .... years; the particular share shall equal ....% of the net profits of the partnership as determined by the partnership's regular accountants. This additional payment has been agreed upon by the partners to represent a payment under and in accordance with Section 736(a)(1) of the 1954 Internal Revenue Code.*

Alternative Article 2. (This provision contemplates payment for good will as a capital asset or "interest in the partnership" in accordance with Section 736(b)(2)(B) of the 1954 Internal Revenue Code, *not* as an income payment under Section 736(a)(2) of the 1954 Internal Revenue Code.) Upon the death or disability of a partner, the partnership shall purchase and the estate of the deceased partner or the disabled partner shall sell his entire interest in the partnership for a price as determined below. It is agreed that the current fair value of the partnership's capital assets as defined in Section 736(b) of the 1954 Internal Revenue Code, including good will, is $............., that the fair value of the accounts receivable, whether billed or unbilled, is $............. and that, therefore, the value of each partner's interest† is as follows:

```
-------------------------------------------- . . . . $-----------
-------------------------------------------- . . . . $-----------
-------------------------------------------- . . . . $-----------
```

The partners agree to redetermine these values within .... days following the end of each (fiscal) (calendar) year, such redetermined values to be endorsed on Schedule A attached hereto and made a part of this agreement. If the partners fail to make such a redetermination of values for a particular year, the last previously stipulated values shall control, except that if the partners fail to make such a redetermination within the .... months immediately preceding the death or onset of disability of a partner, then the values shall be agreed upon by the personal representative of the deceased partner or the disabled partner on the one hand and the remaining partners on behalf of the partnership on the other. If they do not agree to a valuation within .... days after the death or onset of disability of the partner, the value of the deceased or disabled partner's interest shall be determined by arbitration as follows: The remaining partners on behalf of the partnership on the one hand and the representative of the deceased partner or disabled partner on the other shall each name one arbitrator; if the two arbitrators cannot agree upon the values, then the two arbitrators shall appoint a third arbitrator and the decision of the majority shall be

---

* This paragraph provides for payment in lieu of good will as an income item.
† See second footnote on page 69.

binding upon all parties. In determining values by arbitration, (the life insurance proceeds accruing from the policies on the deceased partner's life) (the cash surrender value of the policies of insurance on the life of the disabled partner) (must) (must not) be taken into account; further, an amount for the addition to the good will of the partnership by the deceased or disabled partner of not less than $............. shall be used.

The parties hereto agree and covenant that upon the death or disability of a partner the remaining partners shall continue the partnership business without interruption. Payment of the total purchase price as determined above shall be made with respect to a deceased partner's interest in the partnership in .... equal annual installments, the first such payment to be made .... months from the date of the decedent partner's death. Payment of the total purchase price as determined above shall be made with respect to a disabled partner's interest in the partnership in accordance with the provisions of Article 1 above.

Article 3. The partnership is the applicant and owner of the following life insurance policies issued by National Life Insurance Company:

> Policy #.............insuring the life of ---------------------------
> in the amount of $..............
> Policy #.............insuring the life of ---------------------------
> in the amount of $..............
> Policy #.............insuring the life of ---------------------------
> in the amount of $..............

In addition the partnership is the applicant and owner of the following disability income policies issued by National Life Insurance Company:

> Policy #.............on the life of ----------------------------
> in the amount of $..............
> Policy #.............on the life of ----------------------------
> in the amount of $..............
> Policy #.............on the life of ----------------------------
> in the amount of $..............

The partnership shall designate the Trustee as revocable beneficiary of the above-numbered insurance policies (and all other policies subject to this agreement) to receive the policy proceeds, it being the intention of the parties that the Trustee shall act as escrow. The partnership agrees to pay all premiums on the insurance policies taken out pursuant to this agreement and shall give proof of payment of premiums to the partners whenever any one of them shall so request such proof. If a premium is not paid within 20 days after its due date, the insured shall have the right to pay such premium and be reimbursed therefor by the partnership. The partnership shall have the right to purchase additional insurance on any of the partners; such additional policies shall be listed in Schedule B attached hereto and made a part of this agreement, along with any substitution or withdrawal of insurance policies subject to this agreement. In the event that the partnership decides to purchase additional insurance, each partner hereby agrees to co-operate fully by performing all the requisites of the insurer which are necessary conditions precedent to the issuance of insurance policies. Payment of premiums by the partnership shall be accounted for as an ordinary business expense.*

Article 4. Upon the death or disability of a partner the Trustee, on behalf of the partnership, shall pay the purchase price and make the payments as established by this agreement. The executor or administrator of the estate of the deceased partner or the disabled partner shall execute a bill of sale of his interest in the partnership to the partnership and a waiver of any right of accounting. At the same time the remaining partners shall execute and deliver to the estate of the deceased partner or to the disabled partner an agreement indemnifying the estate of the deceased partner or the disabled partner against all liabilities of the partnership. With respect to a deceased's interest in the partnership, the sale shall take effect as of the close of business on the day of death of the deceased partner and the unpaid balance of the purchase price, except for participation, if any, in profits, shall be evidenced by a series of promissory notes made by the surviving partners on behalf of the partnership to the order of the Trustee; these notes shall provide for the acceleration of the due date of all unpaid notes in default in the payment of any note.

Article 5. Any partner who disposes of his interest in the partnership during his lifetime shall have the right to purchase the policy or policies of insurance on him owned by the partnership or by the co-

---

* Not deductible; see page 50.

partners by paying an amount equal to the interpolated terminal reserve, if any, as of the date of transfer, plus the proportionate part of the gross premium last paid before the date of transfer which covers the period extending beyond that date, less any existing indebtedness charged against the policy or policies. This right shall lapse if not exercised within .... days after such disposal.

Article 6. The partners, the partnership and the personal representative of any deceased partner shall make, execute and deliver any documents necessary or desirable to carry out this agreement.

Article 7. This agreement may be altered, amended or terminated by a writing signed by all of the partners. In the event of a termination of this agreement before the death or disability of a partner, each partner shall be entitled to purchase from the partnership the policy or policies on him upon payment of an amount equal to the interpolated terminal reserve, if any, as of the date of transfer, plus the proportionate part of the gross premium last paid before the date of transfer which covers the period extending beyond that date, less any existing indebtedness charged against the policies.

Article 8. This agreement shall terminate upon the occurance of any of the following events:
(a) Bankruptcy of any partner,
(b) Bankruptcy, receivership or dissolution of the partnership, or
(c) Cessation of the partnership business.
In addition, this agreement shall be null and void if all the partners party hereto die within a period of 30 days.*

---

* Counsel may feel that it would be desirable to treat simultaneous or rapidly successive deaths differently. The close deaths of even two of the three partners raise problems. Let us take an example. If A and B die simultaneously, then under the entity agreement C ends up with ownership of the entire partnership. If the partnership was worth $90,000 while all were alive and the agreement was *fully* funded ($45,000 of insurance on each life), then A's and B's estate, assuming all were equal partners, would each receive $45,000. But because of ballooning (see discussion at page 23 above), i.e., maturation of *two* partnership-owned policies, the value of the partnership upon *two* deaths would be $180,000. One third of $180,000 is $60,000, quite a substantial difference from the one-third value ($45,000) of the partnership if only one partner had died ($135,000). If A and B do not die simultaneously but rather B dies a few moments later, then the problem is similar although the inequity is limited to B's estate only.

Article 9. Notwithstanding the provisions of this agreement, any insurance company whose policies are listed herein or in Schedule B attached hereto is hereby authorized to act in accordance with the terms of any policies issued by it as if this agreement did not exist, and payment or other performance of its contractual obligations by the insurer in accordance with the terms of any such policy shall completely discharge the insurer from all claims and demands of all persons whomsoever. Any insurer is further authorized to provide to an insured partner any information with respect to the policy or policies on him owned by the partnership or by the other partners. No insurer shall be deemed or considered to be a party to this agreement for any purpose.

Article 10. (1) The Trustee agrees to receive and safeguard the insurance policies subject to this agreement, the original copy of this agreement, and all other documents which may be executed in order to carry out the provisions of this agreement. The Trustee shall be under no obligation to make any premium payments on any life or other insurance policies.

(2) Upon the death or disability of a partner, the Trustee shall:

(a) make claim as the designated beneficiary of the insurance policies subject to this agreement to the proceeds of such policies issued with respect on the deceased or disabled partner. The Trustee shall be under no obligation to institute any action to recover the proceeds of any of the policies unless one or more of the partners agrees to indemnify satisfactorily the Trustee for all expenses and attorney's fees connected therewith, and

(b) demand and receive from the remaining partners any promissory notes required to be executed by them as set forth in Article 4 and deliver such notes to the executor, administrator or other legal representative of the deceased. Upon the termination of this agreement, the Trustee shall deliver the insurance policies and other items held by it subject to this agreement back to their respective owners.

Article 11. By mutual agreement in writing, which agreement shall be attached hereto and made a part hereof as Schedule C, the partners and the partnership may remove the Trustee and appoint a new Trustee. The Trustee or any successor Trustee shall resign and discharge itself of the trust by notice in writing to the partners and to the partnership, but such resignation shall not be effective until 30 days after receipt of such written notice. If a Trustee resigns or is removed, the Trustee shall deliver to the successor Trustee all insurance policies and other documents kept by it in accordance with this agreement. A successor Trustee shall have the same rights, duties and powers as the original Trustee. The Trustee shall be paid as compensation a commission of ....% of all amounts paid by the Trustee in the event that a partner should die or become disabled while this agreement is still in force. If this agreement is terminated other than by the death of a partner, the Trustee shall receive a fee of $.............. for its services. The Trustee's commissions or fees, as the case may be, and expenses shall all be paid by the partnership.

Article 12. Except as otherwise expressly stated herein, the partnership agreement heretofore existing among the parties is hereby amended by this agreement the provisions of which shall control. This agreement shall be governed by the law of the State of ....

IN WITNESS WHEREOF the parties hereto have executed this agreement at --, in the County of ------------------------------, State of ------------------------------, on the day and year above written.

------------------------------------   ------------------------------------

                     By ------------------------------------

------------------------------------   ------------------------------------

------------------------------------   ------------------------------------

------------------------------------   ------------------------------------

------------------------------------   -------------------- TRUST COMPANY

                     By ------------------------------------

Specimen Business-Partnership Cross-Purchase Agreement — Disability Provisions — Without Trustee

AGREEMENT made this .... day of ------------------------------, 19........, by and between ----------------------, --------------------- and ---------------------------- co-partners in the ----------------------------- ---------------------------- partnership, and ----------------------------, the partnership.*

WITNESSETH:

WHEREAS ----------------------------, ----------------------------- and ------------------------------------ are co-partners in the business of -------------------------------, and

WHEREAS the interest of each partner in the partnership is as follows:

------------------------- . . . . -------------------------%
------------------------- . . . . -------------------------%
------------------------- . . . . -------------------------%

WHEREAS the primary purpose of this agreement is (1) to provide for the purchase by the remaining partners of the interest of any partner in the partnership in the event of the death or disability of a partner, (2) to provide for the purchase by the remaining partners of the interest of a partner voluntarily withdrawing from the partnership during his lifetime, (3) to provide further for the uninterrupted continuance of the partnership business upon the death or disability of a partner, and (4) to provide the funds necessary to carry out such purchase and sale,

NOW, THEREFORE, in consideration of the mutual agreements and covenants contained herein and for other valuable consideration, receipt of which is hereby acknowledged, it is mutually agreed and covenanted by the partners, each for himself, his heirs, assigns and

---

* The partnership should be party to this instrument if the parties decide that a disabled partner or a decedent partner's successor in interest should participate in partnership earnings and that the partnership should make the payments. To the extent the parties choose this alternative this agreement is hybrid, i.e., partly cross purchase and partly entity purchase.

personal representatives, and by the partnership, and its successors, and by the partnership, for itself as an entity, its successors and assigns, as follows:

Article 1. No partner shall during his lifetime assign, encumber or otherwise dispose of his interest or any part thereof in the partnership, except as provided below:

(1) If a partner should desire to dispose voluntarily of his interest during his lifetime, then he shall first offer in writing to sell his interest to the other partners at the price determined in accordance with the provisions of Article 2 below, provided, however, that such price shall be paid in cash fully on the date of sale, and that the selling partner shall not participate in the future profits of the partnership. Each of such buying partners shall have the right to purchase such portion of the interest as his own interest in the partnership at such date shall bear to the total partnership interest excluding the interest of the selling partner, provided, however, that if any such other partner does not purchase his full proportionate share of the interest being sold, then the balance may be purchased by the other partners equally. If the interest is not purchased by the other partners within .... days of the receipt of the offer to them, then the selling partner may sell it to any other person but shall not sell it without first offering it to the other partners in accordance with the method established above at the price and on the terms offered to such other person if the price is less than the price established by Article 2. If, however, the partnership agreement forming this partnership further restricts, limits or prevents a lifetime sale or transfer by a partner of his interest in the partnership, then such partnership agreement shall prevail notwithstanding the provisions of this Article.

(2) In the event a partner party to this agreement becomes totally and permanently disabled before reaching age 55* and remains so for a period of .... months† from the onset of such disability, then the other partners shall** purchase and

---

* The cut-off age or date should be tied to the limitation, if any, in the funding vehicle.

† This period should be at least as long as the waiting period in the funding insurance; and probably longer.

** This language is mandatory in effect; sometimes an option to purchase is desired by the parties.

the disabled partner shall sell, as of the end of such period, such disabled partner's interest in the partnership in the same proportions as mentioned immediately above. "Disability" or "total and permanent disability" for purposes of this agreement shall be considered that disability of a particular insured partner which is described and determined by the insurer as total and permanent disability in the insurance policies on such insured partner listed in Article 3 below and/or Schedule B attached hereto, provided, however, that no insurer shall be subject to any liability other than its obligations in its policies of insurance. The purchase price shall be that which is established in Article 2 below, provided, however, that such purchase price shall not be paid in a lump sum but instead shall be paid in installments of $............... per month until the total purchase price shall have been paid plus an amount equal to ....% per year of the declining balance of such purchase price. If a disabled partner ceases to be so totally and permanently disabled at some time after such installment payments have commenced but before they have been completed, then* such installments shall be spread out further, namely, at the rate of $............... per month until the balance of said purchase price and interest on the declining balance at the rate of ....% per year shall be wholly paid and satisfied.

Alternative Article 2. (This Article contemplates a payment in lieu of good will as an income item, *not* as a payment for good will under Section 741 of the 1954 Internal Revenue Code.) Upon the death or disability of a partner, the other partners shall purchase and the estate of the deceased partner or the disabled partner shall sell his entire interest in the partnership for a price as determined below. It is agreed that the current fair value of the partnership's capital assets, excluding good will, is $..............., that the fair value of the accounts receivable, whether billed or unbilled, is $..............., that therefore, the value of each partner's interest† is as follows:

---

* This is simply one alternative; the parties could agree to stop the buy-out at such point, or they could even agree to let the disabled partner buy back in again.

† In the interest of simplicity we have assumed no outstanding liabilities of consequence. As a practical matter, however, where liabilities exist an adjustment for them should be made. One should remember that it is important to separate the values of capital and non-capital assets because if the determination is reasonable the Internal Revenue Service is inclined to accept it.

--- · · · · $------------
--- · · · · $------------
--- · · · · $------------

The partners agree to redetermine these values within .... days following the end of each (fiscal) (calendar) year, such redetermined
values to be endorsed on Schedule A attached hereto and made a part
of this agreement. If the partners fail to make such a redetermination
of values for a particular year, the last previously stipulated values shall
control, except that if the partners fail to make such a redetermination
within the .... months immediately preceding the death or onset of
disability of a partner, then the values shall be agreed upon by the personal representative of the deceased partner or the disabled partner on
the one hand and the remaining partners on the other. If they do not
agree to a valuation within .... days after the death or the onset of
disability of the partner, the value of the deceased partner's interest
shall be determined by arbitration as follows: The remaining partners
on the one hand and the representative of the deceased partner or the
disabled partner on the other shall each name one arbitrator; if the
two arbitrators cannot agree upon the value then the two arbitrators
shall appoint a third arbitrator and the decision of the majority shall
be binding upon all parties.

The parties hereto agree and covenant that upon the death or
disability of a partner the remaining partners shall continue the partnership business without interruption. Payment of the total purchase
price as determined above shall be made with respect to a deceased
partner's interest in the partnership in .... equal annual installments, the first such payment to be made within .... months
from the date of the decedent partner's death, the intent of the parties
being that the first payments shall represent payment for the capital
assets, the latter payments for the balance. Payment of the total purchase price as determined above shall be made with respect to a disabled
partner's interest in the partnership in accordance with the provisions
of Article 1 above.

Upon the death or disability of a partner, the surviving partners shall continue the parnership business without interruption and
the estate of the deceased partner or the disabled partner, as the case
may be, shall participate in the net profits of the partnership business
starting on the first day of the month following the date of his death or
the onset of his disability and continuing for a period of .... years;
the particular share shall equal ....% of the net profits of the part-

nership as determined by the partnership's regular accountants. This additional payment has been agreed upon by the partners to represent a payment under and in accordance with Section 736(a)(1) of the 1954 Internal Revenue Code.*

Alternative Article 2. (This provision contemplates payment for good will as a capital asset or "interest in the partnership" in accordance with Section 741 of the 1954 Internal Revenue Code, *not* as an income payment.) Upon the death or disability of a partner, the other partners shall purchase and the estate of the deceased partner or the disabled partner shall sell his entire interest in the partnership for a price as determined below. It is agreed that the current fair value of the partnership's capital assets, including good will, is $..............., that the fair value of the accounts receivable, whether billed or unbilled, is $..............., and that the fair market value of the inventory is $............... and that, therefore, the value of each partner's interest† is as follows:

-- . . . . $...............
-- . . . . $...............
-- . . . . $...............

The partners agree to redetermine these values within .... days following the end of each (fiscal) (calendar) year, such redetermined values to be endorsed on Schedule A attached hereto and made a part of this agreement. If the partners fail to make such a redetermination of values for a particular year, the last previously stipulated values shall control, except that if the partners fail to make such a redetermination within the .... months immediately preceding the death or onset of disability of a partner, then the values shall be agreed upon by the personal representative of the deceased partner or the disabled partner on the one hand and the remaining partners on the other. If they do not agree to a valuation within .... days after the death or onset of disability of the partner, the value of the deceased or disabled partner's interest shall be determined by arbitration as follows: The remaining partners on the one hand and the representative of the deceased partner or the disabled partner on the other shall each name one arbitrator; if the the two arbitrators cannot agree upon

---

* This paragraph provides for payment in lieu of good will as an income item.

† See second footnote on page 79.

the values, then the two arbitrators shall appoint a third arbitrator and the decision of the majority shall be binding upon all parties. In determining values by arbitration, an amount for the addition to the good will of the partnership by the deceased of not less than $............. shall be used.

The parties hereto agree and covenant that upon the death or disability of a partner the remaining partners shall continue the partnership business without interruption. Payment of the total purchase price as determined above shall be made with respect to a deceased partner's interest in the partnership in .... equal annual installments, the first such payment to be made .... months from the date of the decedent partner's death. Payment of the total purchase price as determined above shall be made with respect to a disabled partner's interest in the partnership in accordance with the provisions of Article 1 above.

Article 3. The partners are the applicants, owners and beneficiaries of the following life insurance policies issued by National Life Insurance Company:

Policy #.............insuring the life of ....
in the amount of $............., owned by and payable to ....
....

Policy #.............insuring the life of ....
in the amount of $............., owned by and payable to ....
....

Policy #.............insuring the life of ....
in the amount of $............., owned by and payable to ....
....

Policy #.............insuring the life of ....
in the amount of $............., owned by and payable to ....
....

Policy #.............insuring the life of ....
in the amount of $............., owned by and payable to ....
....

Policy #.............insuring the life of ....
in the amount of $............., owned by and payable to ....
....

In addition the partners are the applicants, owners and beneficiaries of the following disability income policies issued by National Life Insurance Company:

Policy #............on the life of ....
in the amount of $............., owned by and payable to ....
....

Policy #............on the life of ....
in the amount of $............., owned by and payable to ....
....

Policy #............on the life of ....
in the amount of $............., owned by and payable to ....
....

Policy #............on the life of ....
in the amount of $............., owned by and payable to ....
....

Policy #............on the life of ....
in the amount of $............., owned by and payable to ....
....

Policy #............on the life of ....
in the amount of $............., owned by and payable to ....
....

Each partner owning a policy agrees to pay all premiums on the insurance policies owned by him and taken out pursuant to this agreement and shall give proof of payment of premiums to the other partners whenever any one of them shall so request such proof. If a premium is not paid within 20 days after its due date, the insured shall have the right to pay such premium and be reimbursed therefor by the owner-partner. The partners and the partnership shall have the right to purchase any additional insurance on any of the partners; such additional policies shall be listed in Schedule B attached hereto and made a part of this agreement, along with any substitution or withdrawal of insurance policies subject to this agreement. In the event that the partners decide to purchase any additional insurance, each partner hereby agrees to co-operate fully by performing all the requisites of the insurer which are necessary conditions precedent to the issuance of insurance policies.

Article 4. Upon the death or disability of a partner the other partners shall pay the purchase price and make the payments as established by this agreement. The executor or administrator of the estate of the deceased partner or the disabled partner shall execute a bill of sale of his interest in the partnership to the other partners respectively and a waiver of any right of accounting. At the same time the remaining partners shall execute and deliver to the estate of the deceased partner or to the disabled partner an agreement indemnifying the estate of the deceased partner or the disabled partner against all liabilities of the partnership. With respect to a deceased's interest in the partnership, the sale shall take effect as of the close of business on the day of death of the deceased partner and the unpaid balance of the purchase price shall be evidenced by a series of promissory notes made by the several remaining partners to the order of the estate of the deceased; these notes shall provide for the acceleration of the due date of all unpaid notes in default in the payment of any note.

Article 5. Any partner who disposes of his interest in the partnership during his lifetime shall have the right to purchase the policy or policies of insurance on him owned by the partnership or by the other partners by paying an amount equal to the interpolated terminal reserve, if any, as of the date of transfer, plus the proportionate part of the gross premium last paid before the date of transfer which covers the period extending beyond that date, less any existing indebtedness charged against the policy or policies. This right shall lapse if not exercised within .... days after such disposal.

Article 6. The partners, the partnership and the personal representative of any deceased partner shall make, execute and deliver any documents necessary or desirable to carry out this agreement.

Article 7. This agreement may be altered, amended or terminated by a writing signed by all of the partners. In the event of a termination of this agreement before the death or disability of a partner, each partner shall be entitled to purchase from the co-partners the policy or policies on him upon payment of an amount equal to the interpolated terminal reserve, if any, as of the date of transfer, plus the proportionate part of the gross premium last paid before the date of transfer which covers the period extending beyond that date, less any existing indebtedness charged against the policies.

Article 8. This agreement shall terminate upon the occurrence of any of the following events:
  (a) Bankruptcy of any partner,
  (b) Bankruptcy, receivership or dissolution of the partnership, or

(c) Cessation of the partnership business.

In addition, this agreement shall be null and void if all the partners party hereto die within a period of 30 days.*

Article 9. Notwithstanding the provisions of this agreement, any insurance company whose policies are listed herein or in Schedule B attached is hereby authorized to act in accordance with the terms of any policies issued by it as if this agreement did not exist, and payment or other performance of its contractual obligations by the insurer in accordance with the terms of any such policy shall completely discharge the insurer from all claims and demands of all persons whomsoever. Any insurer is further authorized to provide to an insured partner any information with respect to the policy or policies on him owned by the partnership or by the co-partners. No insurer shall be deemed or considered to be a party to this agreement for any purpose.

Article 10. The partners further agree hereby that upon the death or disability of one of them the remaining partners will cause this partnership to make the election provided for under Section 754 of the 1954 Internal Revenue Code so that the basis of partnership property shall be adjusted to reflect the payments made hereunder.

Article 11. Except as otherwise expressly stated herein, the partnership agreement heretofore existing among the parties is hereby amended by this agreement the provisions of which shall control. This agreement shall be governed by the law of the State of

IN WITNESS WHEREOF the parties hereto have executed this agreement at --, in the County of

---

* Counsel may feel that it would be desirable to treat simultaneous or rapidly successive deaths differently. The close deaths of even two of the three partners raise problems. Let us take an example. If A and B die simultaneously, then under the cross-purchase plan C ends up with an obligation to buy out both of them. But if the partnership was worth $90,000 while all were alive and assuming that each one had *fully* funded his obligations with respect to buying a prorata share of the interest of each of the others (e.g., C purchased a $15,000 policy on A and a $15,000 policy on B, A $15,000 each on C and B, etc.), then C will not have enough money to pay fully both estates. If A and B do not simultaneously but rather B dies shortly after A, then, while C will have sufficient proceeds to pay A's estate, C will have nowhere near enough to pay B's estate.

-------------------------------------, State of -------------------------------, on the day and year above written.

-------------------------------------   ---*

                           By -------------------------------------

-------------------------------------   ---

-------------------------------------   ---

-------------------------------------   ---

*See footnote on page 77.

Specimen Business-Partnership Cross-Purchase Agreement — Disability Provisions — With Trustee

AGREEMENT made this .... day of ----------------------------------, 19........., by and between ----------------------------, ---------------------- and ---------------------------------- co-partners in the ---------------------------- ---------------------------------- partnership, ----------------------------------, the partnership,* and the ---------------------------- Trust Company, a ---------------------------- Corporation (hereinafter called "Trustee").

WITNESSETH:

WHEREAS ----------------------------, ------------------------------ and -- are co-partners in the business of ----------------------------------, and

WHEREAS the interest of each partner in the partnership is as follows:

------------------------------ · · · · ------------------------%
------------------------------ · · · · ------------------------%
------------------------------ · · · · ------------------------%

WHEREAS the primary purpose of this agreement is (1) to provide for the purchase by the remaining partners of the interest of any partner in the partnership in the event of the death or disability of a partner, (2) to provide for the purchase by the remaining partners of the interest of a partner voluntarily withdrawing from the partnership during his lifetime, (3) to provide further for the uninterrupted continuance of the partnership business upon the death or disability of a partner, and (4) to provide the funds necessary to carry out such purchase and sale,

NOW, THEREFORE, in consideration of the mutual agreements and covenants contained herein and for other valuable consideration,

---

* The partnership should be party to this instrument if the parties decide that a disabled partner or a decedent partner's successor-in-interest should participate in partnership earnings and that the partnership should make the payments. To the extent the parties choose this alternative this agreement is hybrid, i.e., partly cross purchase and partly entity purchase.

receipt of which is hereby acknowledged, it is mutually agreed and covenanted by the partners, each for himself, his heirs, assigns and personal representatives, and by the partnership, for itself as an entity, its successors and assigns, as follows:

Article 1. No partner shall during his lifetime assign, encumber or otherwise dispose of his interest or any part thereof in the partnership, except as provided below:

(1) If a partner should desire to dispose voluntarily of his interest during his lifetime, then he shall first offer in writing to sell his interest to the other partners at the price determined in accordance with the provisions of Article 2 below, provided, however, that such price shall be paid in cash, fully on the date of sale, and that the selling partner shall not participate in the future profits of the partnership. Each of such buying partners shall have the right to purchase such portion of the interest as his own interest in the partnership at such date shall bear to the total partnership interest excluding the interest of the selling partner, provided, however, that if any such other partner does not purchase his full proportionate share of the interest being sold, then the balance may be purchased by the other partners equally. If the interest is not purchased by the other partners within .... days of the receipt of the offer to them, then the selling partner may sell it to any other person but shall not sell it without first offering it to the other partners in accordance with the method established above at the price and on the terms offered to such other person if the price is less than the price established by Article 2. If, however, the partnership agreement forming this partnership further restricts, limits or prevents a lifetime sale or transfer by a partner of his interest in the partnership, then such partnership agreement shall prevail notwithstanding the provisions of this Article.

(2) In the event a partner party to this agreement becomes totally and permanently disabled before reaching age 55,* and remains so for a period of .... months† from the onset of

---

* The cut-off age or date should be tied to the limitation, if any, in the funding vehicle.

† This period should be at least as long as the waiting period in the funding insurance, and probably longer.

such disability, then the other partners shall* purchase and the disabled partner shall sell, as of the end of such period, such disabled partner's interest in the partnership in the same proportions as mentioned immediately above. "Disability" or "total and permanent disability" for purposes of this agreement shall be considered that disability of a particular insured partner which is described and determined by the insurer as total and permanent disability in the insurance policies on such insured partner listed in Article 3 below and/or Schedule B attached hereto, provided, however, that no insurer shall be subject to any liability other than its obligations in its policies of insurance. The purchase price shall be that which is established in Article 2 below, provided, however, that such purchase price shall not be paid in a lump sum but instead shall be paid in installments of $............. per month until the total purchase price shall have been paid plus an amount equal to ....% per year of the declining balance of such purchase price. If a disabled partner ceases to be so totally and permanently disabled at some time after such installment payments have commenced but before they have been completed, then† such installments shall be spread out further, namely, at the rate of $............. per month until the balance of said purchase price and interest on the declining balance at the rate of ....% per year shall be wholly paid and satisfied.

Alternative Article 2. (This Article contemplates a payment in lieu of good will as an income item, *not* as a payment for good will under Section 741 of the 1954 Internal Revenue Code.) Upon the death or disability of a partner, the other partners shall purchase and the estate of the deceased partner or the disabled partner shall sell his entire interest in the partnership for a price as determined below. It is agreed that the current fair value of the partnership's capital assets, excluding good will, is $............., that the fair value of the accounts receivable, whether billed or unbilled, is $............., that the fair market value of the inventory is $............. and that, therefore, the

---

* This language is mandatory in effect; sometimes an option to purchase is desired by the parties.

† This is simply one alternative; the parties could agree to stop the buy-out at such point, or they could even agree to let the disabled partner buy back in again.

value of each partner's interest* is as follows:

-- · · · · $------------

-- · · · · $------------

-- · · · · $------------

     The partners agree to redetermine these values within .... days following the end of each (fiscal) (calendar) year, such redetermined values to be endorsed on Schedule A attached hereto and made a part of this agreement. If the partners fail to make such a redetermination of values for a particular year, the last previously stipulated values shall control, except that if the partners fail to make such a redetermination within the .... months immediately preceding the death or onset of disability of a partner, then the values shall be agreed upon by the personal representative of the deceased partner or the disabled partner on the one hand and the remaining partners on the other. If they do not agree to a valuation within .... days after the death or the onset of disability of the partner, the value of the deceased or disabled partner's interest shall be determined by arbitration as follows: The remaining partners on the one hand and the representative of the deceased partner or the disabled partner on the other shall each name one arbitrator; if the two arbitrators cannot agree upon the value then the two arbitrators shall appoint a third arbitrator and the decision of the majority shall be binding upon all parties.

     The parties hereto agree and covenant that upon the death or disability of a partner the remaining partners shall continue the partnership business without interruption. Payment of the total purchase price as determined above shall be made with respect to a deceased partner's interest in the partnership in .... equal annual installments, the first such payment to be made within .... months from the date of the decedent partner's death, the intent of the parties being that the first payments shall represent payment for the capital assets, the latter payments for the balance. Payment of the total purchase price as determined above shall be made with respect to a disabled partner's interest in the partnership in accordance with the provisions of Article 1 above.

---

* In the interest of simplicity we have assumed no outstanding liabilities of consequence. As a practical matter, however, where liabilities exist an adjustment for them should be made. One should remember that it is important to separate the values of capital and non-capital assets because if the determination is reasonable the Internal Revenue Service is inclined to accept it.

Upon the death or disability of a partner, the surviving partners shall continue the parnership business without interruption and the estate of the deceased partner or the disabled partner, as the case may be, shall participate in the net profits of the partnership business starting on the first day of the month following the date of his death or the onset of his disability and continuing for a period of .... years; the particular share shall equal ....% of the net profits of the partnership as determined by the partnership's regular accountants. This additional payment has been agreed upon by the partners to represent a payment under and in accordance with Section 736(a)(1) of the 1954 Internal Revenue Code.*

Alternative Article 2. (This provision contemplates payment for good will as a capital asset or "interest in the partnership" in accordance with Section 741 of the 1954 Internal Revenue Code, *not* as an income payment.) Upon the death or disability of a partner, the other partners shall purchase and the estate of the deceased partner or the disabled partner shall sell his entire interest in the partnership for a price as determined below. It is agreed that the current fair value of the partnership's capital assets, including good will, is $............., that the fair value of the accounts receivable, whether billed or unbilled, is $............., and that the fair market value of the inventory is $............. and that, therefore, the value of each partner's interest† is as follows:

-- · · · · $............

-- · · · · $............

-- · · · · $............

The partners agree to redetermine these values within .... days following the end of each (fiscal) (calendar) year, such redetermined values to be endorsed on Schedule A attached hereto and made a part of this agreement. If the partners fail to make such a redetermination of values for a particular year, the last previously stipulated values shall control, except that if the partners fail to make such a redetermination within the .... months immediately preceding the death or onset of disability of a partner, then the values shall be agreed upon by the personal representative of the deceased partner or disabled partner on the

---

* This paragraph provides for payment in lieu of good will as an income item.

† See footnote on page 90.

one hand and the remaining partners on the other. If they do not agree to a valuation within .... days after the death or onset of disability of the partner, the value of the deceased or disabled partner's interest shall be determined by arbitration as follows: The remaining partners on the one hand and the representative of the deceased partner or the disabled partner on the other shall each name one arbitrator; if the the two arbitrators cannot agree upon the values, then the two arbitrators shall appoint a third arbitrator and the decision of the majority shall be binding upon all parties. In determining values by arbitration, an amount for the addition to the good will of the partnerhip by the deceased of not less than $.............. shall be used.

The parties hereto agree and covenant that upon the death or disability of a partner the remaining partners shall continue the partnership business without interruption. Payment of the total purchase price as determined above shall be made with respect to a deceased partner's interest in the partnership in .... equal annual installments, the first such payment to be made within .... months from the date of the decedent partner's death. Payment of the total purchase price as determined above shall be made with respect to a disabled partner's interest in the partnership in accordance with the provisions of Article 1 above.

Article 3. The partners are the applicants and owners of the following life insurance policies issued by National Life Insurance Company:

Policy #............insuring the life of ....
in the amount of $.............., owned by ....
and payable to the .... Trust Company.

Policy #............insuring the life of ....
in the amount of $.............., owned by ....
and payable to the .... Trust Company.

Policy #............insuring the life of ....
in the amount of $.............., owned by ....
and payable to the .... Trust Company.

Policy #............insuring the life of ....
in the amount of $.............., owned by ....
and payable to the .... Trust Company.

Policy #............insuring the life of ....
in the amount of $.............., owned by ....
and payable to the .... Trust Company.

Policy #.............insuring the life of ....
in the amount of $............., owned by ....
and payable to the .... Trust Company.

In addition the partners are the applicants and owners of the following disability income policies issued by National Life Insurance Company:

Policy #............. on the life of ....
in the amount of $............., and payable to the ....
Trust Company.

Policy #............. on the life of ....
in the amount of $............., and payable to the ....
Trust Company.

Policy #............. on the life of ....
in the amount of $............., and payable to the ....
Trust Company.

Policy #............. on the life of ....
in the amount of $............., and payable to the ....
Trust Company.

Policy #............. on the life of ....
in the amount of $............., and payable to the ....
Trust Company.

Policy #............. on the life of ....
in the amount of $............., and payable to the ....
Trust Company.

Each partner owning a policy or policies agrees to pay all premiums on the insurance policies owned by him and taken out pursuant to this agreement and shall give proof of payment of premiums to the other partners whenever any one of them shall so request such proof. If a premium is not paid within 20 days after its due date, the insured shall have the right to pay such premium and be reimbursed therefor by the owner-partner. The partners and the partnership shall have the right to purchase any additional insurance on any of the partners; such additional policies shall be listed in Schedule B attached hereto and made a part of this agreement, along with any substitution or withdrawal of insurance policies subject to this agreement. In the event that the partners decide to purchase any additional insurance, each partner hereby agrees to co-operate fully by performing all the requisites of the insurer which are necessary conditions precedent to the issuance of insurance policies.

Article 4. Upon the death or disability of a partner, the Trustee shall pay the purchase price and make the payments as established by this agreement. The executor or administrator of the estate of the deceased partner or the disabled partner shall execute a bill of sale of his interest in the partnership to the other partners respectively and a waiver of any right of accounting. At the same time the remaining partners shall execute and deliver to the estate of the deceased partner or to the disabled partner against all liabilities of the partnership. With respect to a deceased's interest in the partnership, the sale shall take effect as of the close of business on the day of death of the deceased partner and the unpaid balance of the purchase price shall be evidenced by a series of promissory notes made by the several remaining partners to the order of the Trustee; these notes shall provide for the acceleration of the due date of all unpaid notes in the series in default in the payment of any note.

Article 5. Any partner who disposes of his interest in the partnership during his lifetime shall have the right to purchase the policy or policies of insurance on him owned by the partnership or by the co-partners by paying an amount equal to the interpolated terminal reserve, if any, as of the date of transfer, plus the proportionate part of the gross premium last paid before the date of transfer which covers the period extending beyond that date, less any existing indebtedness charged against the policy or policies. This right shall lapse if not exercised within .... days after such disposal.

Article 6. The partners, the partnership and the personal representative of any deceased partner shall make, execute and deliver any documents necessary or desirable to carry out this agreement.

Article 7. This agreement may be altered, amended or terminated by a writing signed by all of the partners. In the event of a termination of this agreement before the death or disability of a partner, each partner shall be entitled to purchase from the co-partners or the partnership the policy or policies on him upon payment of an amount equal to the interpolated terminal reserve, if any, as of the date of transfer, plus the proportionate part of the gross premium last paid before the date of transfer which covers the period extending beyond that date, less any existing indebtedness charged against the policies.

Article 8. This agreement shall terminate upon the occurrence of any of the following events:

(a) Bankruptcy of any partner,

(b) Bankruptcy, receivership or dissolution of the partnership, or

(c) Cessation of the partnership business.

In addition, this agreement shall be null and void if all the partners party hereto die within a period of 30 days.*

Article 9. Notwithstanding the provisions of this agreement, any insurance company whose policies are listed herein or in Schedule B attached hereto is hereby authorized to act in accordance with the terms of any policies issued by it as if this agreement did not exist, and payment or other performance of its contractual obligations by the insurer in accordance with the terms of any such policy shall completely discharge the insurer from all claims and demands of all persons whomsoever. Any insurer is further authorized to provide to an insured partner any information with respect to the policy or policies on him owned by the partnership or by the co-partners. No insurer shall be deemed or considered to be a party to this agreement for any purpose.

Article 10. The duties of the Trustee are as follows:

(1) To receive and hold safely the insurance policies subject to this agreement, the original copy of this cross-purchase agreement and any other documents which may be executed and delivered to the Trustee to carry out the provisions of this agreement.

(2) Upon the death or disability of a partner

(a) to make claim as the designated beneficiary of the insurance policies subject to this agreement to the proceeds of the policies issued on the deceased or disabled

---

* Counsel may feel that it would be desirable to treat simultaneous or rapidly successive deaths differently. The close deaths of even two of the three partners raise problems. Let us take an example, If A and B die simultaneously, then under the cross-purchase plan C ends up with an obligation to buy out both of them. But if the partnership was worth $90,000 while all were alive and assuming that each one had *fully* funded his obligations with respect to buying a prorata share of the interest of each of the others (e.g., C purchased a $15,000 policy on A and a $15,000 policy on B, A $15,000 each on C and B, etc.), then C will not have enough money to pay fully both estates. If A and B do not die simultaneously but rather B dies shortly after A, then, while C will have sufficient proceeds to pay A's estate, C will have nowhere near enough to pay B's estate.

partner. The Trustee shall be under no obligation to institute any action to recover the proceeds of any of the policies unless the remaining partner satisfactorily indemnifies the Trustee for all expenses and attorney's fees connected therewith;

(b) to demand and receive from the remaining partners any promissory notes required to be executed as set forth in Article 4 and to deliver such notes to the executor, administrator or other legal representative of the deceased partner or to the disabled partner.

(3) Upon termination of this agreement other than in conjunction with a sale of a partnership interest as herein provided, the Trustee shall deliver the policies subject to this agreement to their respective owners.

(4) The Trustee shall be under no obligation to make any premium payments on any of the life insurance policies subject to this agreement.

Article 11. The Trustee shall be paid as compensation a commission of ....% of all amounts paid by the Trustee in the event that a partner should die or become disabled while this agreement is still in force. If this agreement is terminated other than by the death or disablity of a partner, the Trustee shall receive a fee of $............. for its services. The Trustee's commissions or fees, as the case may be, and expenses shall be divided and paid equally by the remaining partners.

Article 12. The partners further agree hereby that upon the death or disability of one of them the remaining partners will cause the partnership to make the election provided for under Section 754 of the 1954 Internal Revenue Code so that the basis of partnership property shall be adjusted to reflect the payments made hereunder.

Article 13. Except as otherwise expressly stated herein, the partnership agreement heretofore existing among the parties is hereby amended by this agreement the provisions of which shall control. This agreement shall be governed by the law of the State of ....

IN WITNESS WHEREOF the parties hereto have executed this agreement at --, in the County of ----------------------------, State of ----------------------------, on the day and year above written.

---------------------------------------   ---------------------------------------*

                                                   By ---------------------------------------

---------------------------------------   ---------------------------------------

---------------------------------------   ---------------------------------------

---------------------------------------   ---------------------------------------

---------------------------------------   ---------------------------------------

---------------------------------------   --------------------- TRUST COMPANY

                                                   By ---------------------------------------

---

* See footnote on page 87.